# CODA

Simon Gray was born in 1936. He began his writing career with *Colmain* (1963), the first of five novels, all published by Faber. He is the author of many plays for TV and radio, also films, including the 1987 adaptation of J. L. Carr's *A Month in the Country*, and TV films including *Running Late*, *After Pilkington* (winner of the Prix Italia) and Emmy Award-winning *Unnatural Pursuits*. He wrote more than thirty stage plays, among them *Butley* and *Otherwise Engaged* (which both received *Evening Standard* Awards for Best Play), *Close of Play*, *The Rear Column*, *Quartermaine's Terms*, *The Common Pursuit*, *Hidden Laughter*, *The Late Middle Classes* (winner of the Barclay's Best Play Award), *Japes*, *The Old Masters* (his ninth play to be directed by Harold Pinter) and *Little Nell*, which premiered at the Theatre Royal Bath in 2007, directed by Peter Hall. *Little Nell* was first broadcast on BBC Radio 4 in 2006, and *Missing Dates* in 2008. His play *The Last Cigarette*, which he adapted with Hugh Whitemore from *The Smoking Diaries*, premiered in March 2009. In 1991 he was made BAFTA Writer of the Year. His acclaimed works of non-fiction include *An Unnatural Pursuit*, *How's That for Telling 'Em, Fat Lady?* and, published by Granta, *Fat Chance*, *Enter a Fox*, *The Smoking Diaries*, *The Year of the Jouncer* and *The Last Cigarette*. He was appointed CBE in the 2005 New Year's Honours for his services to drama and literature. Simon Gray died in August 2008.

Praise for *Coda*:

'Caustic honest, a disarming kind of wide-eyed world-weariness, fury tempered by comedy (and vice versa) and a wholly original look-no-hands prose style, free-wheeling yet at the same time expertly balanced and controlled. And also, perhaps above

everything else, Gray has that unfakeable quality of lovability: reading Simon Gray's diaries is such an intimate, companionable experience that somehow he makes you feel as though you are inside his mind, and that he is inside yours.'

Craig Brown, *Mail on Sunday*

'The effortless, rambling style he's accidentally found himself cultivating here reaches its zenith . . . He finishes not in ugly mid-sentence but clearly, cleanly, perfectly. A casually perfect but unexpectedly painful early full stop to a life and a mind for which we are immeasurably richer.'

Euan Ferguson, *Observer*

'The heartbreaking thing about *Coda* is that it is Simon Gray at his very best . . . It is an effortlessly astonishing piece of writing that establishes Gray without a doubt among the great autobiographers . . . Oh Simon Gray! I don't usually pay much attention to quotations from reviews on book jackets, but every fond and admiring word on the back of the jacket of *Coda* is absolutely true.'

Diana Athill, *Literary Review*

'In the final analysis that the death of a writer inevitably invites, the diaries not only benefit from his experience as a playwright in terms of dramatic immediacy and compression, but also proved the perfect vehicle for the expression of the full range of his unique personality and wit – I would say "genius" were that not such a loaded word.'

Tony Gould, *Spectator*

'*Coda* is a victory of tone. Gray remains himself throughout, undiminished, always truthful, both observant and self-observant. Although describing terminal illness, it is an assertion of life, pleasurable to read, deeply companionable, despite the physical humiliations detailed. *Coda* is as good as anything he ever wrote.'

David Sexton, *Evening Standard*

# SIMON GRAY

# Coda

*faber and faber*

GRANTA

First published in 2008 by
Faber and Faber Ltd
Bloomsbury House
74–77 Great Russell Street
London WC1B 3DA
and
Granta
12 Addison Avenue
London W11 4QR

This paperback edition first published in 2009

Typeset by Faber and Faber Ltd
Printed in England by CPI Bookmarque, Croydon

A CIP record for this book
is available from the British Library

ISBN 978–1–84708–100–1

**Mixed Sources**
Product group from well-managed
forests and other controlled sources
www.fsc.org  Cert no. TT-COC-002227
© 1996 Forest Stewardship Council
FSC

2 4 6 8 10 9 7 5 3 1

*Victoria – without whom, nothing*

# London

# Grinner with a Knife

It's coming up to 4 a.m. on a Friday morning, and I've just promised myself, a self loaded with and lightened by a couple of sleeping pills, that I will go on with this tomorrow – just get a first sentence, I told myself, and when you are ready tomorrow look at it, and then continue into another sentence, and if you can another one, and if you're lucky you'll catch up with yourself in what you understand, at 4 a.m. on this Friday morning, will be an account of what you've been told, on good medical authority, is the beginning of your dying.

*A demain*, therefore.

*Demain* has arrived, and I'm going on with this, the beginning of my dying – now, is that merely a perverse way of writing the end of my living – the ending of my life? I don't think so – the perverse part of my situation is that, apart from the fact – not yet completely authenticated – that I'm dying, I feel really quite well, physically better than I've felt in a long time, for the last year almost, so really it's not that I'm dying, rather that I'm being killed off by a tumour that so far hasn't announced itself by an overt presence on its host – my body, more specifically my lung – but has been discovered –

It's like this, at least in my imagination – you come back home one evening, the house is dark, as you expect it to be, you switch on a light, an extra light, one you didn't know you had, and unexpectedly your eye goes to a corner of the room that you've never seen illuminated before, and in it is crouching a grinning man holding a knife – and then the light goes off, normal lighting is resumed, there is no one in the corner as far as you can see, but you know that if the light came on again you would see him again, see him in more detail, the teeth, one particular and prominent tooth, the completely confident intent in the eyes, the compactness, wholeness, distinctive of his intent to murder you – and you can't get out of your house, which was once your protection and the most comforting place in the world – it is now your prison, inhabited by you and the creature in the corner, who might also be slipping into other rooms, to catch you there, or there, or there – in his own good time. You are his good time, in waiting. So I am living in a state of terror and cowardice – I am waiting to be murdered in my house by the grinning murderer with the knife – that is sort of how I feel about the tumour in my lung. Almost I want to give myself over to him – there, there you are, do it, do it now – but

4

mostly I want to run and run, as if running will carry me away from him, and not carry him along inside me, there for the ride, enjoying it.

## A Run in the Churchyard

And indeed an hour or so ago I went to the church-yard at the end of our street, unlocked the gate, and walked around and around for an hour without stop-ping, a very rapid plod, head lowered so I don't have to meet the look of anyone else strolling along the paths, keeping my eyes off any dogs with affection-ate, trouser-pawing tendencies – I felt my body surg-ing along, even if rightly I've called it a plod, I felt a looseness in my legs, an easy swing in my arms, and at one point, having made sure that there was no wit-ness but a bunched-up woman with two corgi-type dogs who was as determined to avoid me as I was to avoid her, I went to the top of the path and set out on a jog. It was as if I'd never run before in my life.

I feel a need to interpolate here a brief history of my athletic career, which entails, I think, a brief his-tory of my mother's career – she was a fine athlete, outstanding in the broad jump, a competition long ago eliminated as an international event – you stood still on a board embedded in the ground, swung your arms, heaved yourself through the air into a pit of sand – a stationary version of the long jump, which involves a very fast sprint to a board embedded in the ground, from which you take off into a pit of sand – Mummy also did that, the long jump, as well as the high jump, and won some medals at international level – there was a photograph in an album of her receiving a medal from the King of Sweden, not long before the last war, although I can't remember for which event, or whether it was gold, silver or bronze – but anyway there she was in the photograph, a medal-winner and acknowledged as such by Swedish royalty – I have an idea that it was King Gustav, but have no idea whether Sweden ever had a king called Gustav, it's just that the name Gustav has attached itself to the memory of a small man with a beard holding something out to Mummy, who is stooped in a sort of bow – but what was she wearing? I have a memory of her position but not of her clothes – I wonder what happened to the photograph, and how old I was when I saw it – I do remember clearly that it embarrassed us, Nigel, my older brother, and me – we didn't like looking at it, or hearing about her athletic achievements, they seemed inappropriate for a mother, even a long-legged mother who swam and played tennis, and would race after us to deliver a kick or a blow, up and down the stairs or across the garden – I've described elsewhere her combative nature, her readiness to meet perceived impertinence or foolishness with a cuff or a kick, and how, after five years of separation – we were evacuated to Canada during the war when I was three, Nigel four – we relished the excitement and drama she brought into our lives, as well as the reassuring intimacy of casual and only accidentally painful violence – when our reflexes failed, for instance, and we stumbled into rather than away from the swiping hand.

But the idea of her running about and jumping in public was strange and distasteful, her winning medals somehow made it worse, it seemed much more respectable and normal that she'd been a gym teacher and coached lacrosse and hockey at a girls' school until she met and married my father, a Canadian doctor, a locum at her father's practice – actually he was engaged to her sister until Mummy returned from her school in Shropshire and took him for herself – but why am I going back into all this history? I've already written about it elsewhere – I think to establish that being good at running and jumping, football and cricket was in my genes, and that the memory of being good seemed to be lingering in my body like a taunt, as if my legs themselves had a memory of a time when they could lift and stretch, and I could fly along the top of the ground with no need of muscles or bones or lungs, all those parts of me that have become more and more notice-able as they've served me less and less well, like bad waiters – a ridiculous analogy, it would make my body into a restaurant, but it gets me back to the sentence that I interrupted about being in the church-yard just a few hours ago feeling that I could walk, was in fact walking, with power and authority, so how could I be terminally ill? and deciding to test myself further with a little run – and I tried, and – I wrote – 'It was as if I'd never run before' and really the sentence should have gone on 'which is proba-bly why I couldn't do it', because the fact is that I couldn't, not even for three steps, for all my legs' memory of once having sped and flown etc., they'd forgotten – I've forgotten – how to run.

I tried to work it out, the mechanics of it, and after a bit of lifting my legs and pumping my arms while stationary, I tottered forward and managed a jerky little passage of about fifteen steps of something that was more complicated and more urgent than a walk, but also made me feel ill with exhaustion and shame, as if I'd been struggling uphill with a great weight, which was I suppose the weight of my self, accumu-lated over seven decades – I thought I must get home and lie down, and headed towards the gate, which the two-corgis woman seemed to be holding open for me but wasn't, she was holding it open for her dogs, just as I got to it she let it swing closed behind her, and hurried off with her head down, the dogs scampering playfully around her, and I had to fumble for my key, locate the lock, heave it open – and here I am, having rested on the bed for a while, writing it all down and thinking as I do so that this is not the way a man should confront the fact that he's dying, how can writing of his failure to run about in the local churchyard possibly help him, and what if I'd succeeded? What if I'd sped and flown up and down the paths as once I could have done, once, once upon a time I could have done?

## A Short History of Failure

I keep sitting down to go on with this, again and again and again, night after night after night, but it's no good. I suppose that I'm the writing equivalent of dumb-struck.

It's been weeks now – a month even, the whole of July, and I still can't do it.

That's August gone, the summer almost over. I haven't the will is the truth of the matter. Perhaps it's been zapped by the radiotherapy. Every time I pick up my pen I write into my yellow pad either a squiggle or that I can't write, and put the pen down again.

We've planned to go to Crete. In fact we should have been there on Friday, and then again yesterday, but I wasn't well enough – washed out and frail, the effect of the radiotherapy. We're now booked on a flight tomorrow afternoon. If we get there perhaps I'll be able to put something down.

OK, here we are, and I'll try. The thing is, it's all so haphazard in memory that I can't do it chronologically, or in any sort of order, probably, I'll just have to let it happen as it happens. If it happens.

Well now.
    Take it easy.
    Go from where you're sitting, why not?
    Yes, but not today.
    Tomorrow. I'll start tomorrow.

As it happens, then.

It's tomorrow again.

So tomorrow I'll start. Tomorrow I'll let it happen as it happens.

# Crete

# As It Happens at Last

As it happens, I am sitting at a long blue table with my back cushioned against the wall of a small white chapel. I think this table is actually a part of a restaurant and not the chapel, because just beyond it are small, square tables with canvas chairs, some of them under a makeshift roof, and then there is a kitchen and a section enclosed to make a dining room, and an outside grill and bar arrangement – so really, while all the currently highly sensitive and emotional part of me clings to the notion that I've attached myself physically to a chapel, the truth is likely to be that I'm sitting in an empty restaurant. I've been pretending I don't know it's a restaurant, that really it's a complicated extension of the chapel, serving a religious function for the feasts of the saints' name days, for example, and that all the people of the neighbourhood attend it and then eat appropriate dishes, or eat appropriate dishes before attending it, served by assigned parishioners or members of a holy order, but it's no good, the fact is that I ate here myself, last night, with Victoria of course. The food was delicious, at least Victoria says it was, and actually I did manage to eat a little of it

– eating is a bit tricky at the moment as a) I'm a bit short of an appetite since the radiotherapy and b) I seem to have lost my sense of taste since the radiotherapy and c) I have trouble fitting my dentures into my mouth since the radiotherapy – it's as if my lower and upper jaw have been realigned by the rays to give me a differently shaped mouth from the one my dentist worked from. On the other hand I could see that the food was at least popular, because everybody at the surrounding tables ate it with real enthusiasm, and made appreciative if charmless noises – grunting and going 'mmmm'. There was a French couple at the table next to ours, neat and low-voiced, young middle-aged and gravely happy – he looked a bit smooth and film-starry until he suddenly addressed the waiter on the subject of the pieces of cheese fried in batter they'd just consumed – his clear, tight little film-starry face became vulpine, you could see all his teeth – such was his grinning enthusiasm for the pieces of fried cheese in batter, a Crete speciality, apparently, and offered as a pudding because the batter is soaked in honey. His wife or mistress was a charming though not very pretty mess of a woman, farouche might be the word, short black hair tangled, and the sleeves of her wind-breaker down over her wrists. She was, like him, a hearty and appreciative eater. They were both heavy smokers. It was what I noticed first about them. During the course of the meal she had five, he had four, cigarettes, but the odd thing was that they shared the pack – no, she was the keeper of the pack, kept it just above her plate, and he would reach over, take the pack, shake out a cigarette, light it with the lighter she kept on top of the pack, then put both back in front of her. In my experience, heavy smokers like to have their own pack and lighter, so there was probably something symbolic in their arrangement. He liked the sense of her being in charge, she liked the sense of being his handmaiden. I don't think it was simply that he'd forgotten his cigarettes and lighter, it looked habitual, a relaxed and intimate ritual that might one day, when recollected by one or other of them, be charged with pathos, even grief.

It was very pleasant and peaceful sitting under the Cretan night sky, the sound of the waves lapping at the beach below, the murmur of voices and quiet laughter, well, that is until a trio of elderly northerners, Yorkshire from their accents, suddenly appeared and sat down at a table near us – two women and a man with a finely structured, noble face, with crinkly eyes and a furrowed brow who looked unnervingly like Sean Connery – the impersonation helped by the grey spade beard, heavy eyebrows and balding head, but in his speech, in the level of his conversation – it's not simply that he was boastful and loud but he appeared to be retarded in some way. I don't believe he was drunk, but he shouted and bellowed out laughter as if he were in a crowded pub. At one point he told a joke that involved imitating a hen, so he 'did' the hen with flappings of his arms and squawks and bouncings up and down in his chair – the two women, one of whom could be mistaken for an academic – cropped grey hair, serious spectacles, a blinking, murmuring manner, short and squat of figure, but with a piercing laugh that, once started, went on and on – the other was fat, slovenly, coarse-haired, hoarse-voiced – the three of them, especially when they were simultaneously in full flow, the two women screaming out their laughter, he raising his voice to be heard above it, seemed to have come from a mid-twentieth century that only existed in the cinema and in novels – *Saturday Night and Sunday Morning, Room at the Top* and so forth, and yet here they were last night at a table a few yards away from the little chapel, against the wall of which I'm resting my back as I write this –

My tendency is to go on writing this, and this sort of stuff – about the hotel, its restaurants, the sea, Crete, to which we've come in late September – as a way of avoiding what is most on my mind to write about, which is that I have a year to live. No, three months ago I was told that I had a year to live, so now I have nine months to live. Well, medical predictions, even when delivered with an off-hand matter-of-factness, can't surely be precise even to the month. Everybody knows somebody who knows somebody who was given six months to live, and here they are, only just dead, eight years later. Or, in exceptional cases, here they still are, eating oysters and boring the shit out of people. Eight years, I've noticed, tends to be the outer limit of an incorrect prognosis. There was that remarkable woman who died a few weeks or so ago, she rode bicycles around the world, took part in marathons, walked across continents, all while undergoing chemotherapy etc. and had only just completed some astonishing run or walk or cycle three days before she died, which was eight years later than had been authorised for her. One wonders how the doctor who made the prognosis felt about her continued, and very public – often saluted in headlines – survival. Did he feel a bit of a charlie, and harbour dark thoughts, especially at the beginning of her so-to-speak post-mortem career, find himself wishing, and then willing, her out of the newspapers and off the television screens into the spot he'd assigned to

17

her? I don't think the prognosticating doctor's name was ever mentioned – a pity, really, it would have been amusing to read that 'Julia Hobday, who seven years ago was told by Dr Angus McDuff of the Middlebury Cancer Hospital that she would be dead in six months, came fourth in yesterday's Chelsea–St Ives Marathon. Dr McDuff, when asked for his comment, said that –'

Well, what would he say? 'I'm only human' is the currently favoured excuse for failure. Footballers offer it after losing football matches, politicians after costing lives, journalists after ruining reputations, policemen after mowing you down in their pandas, and I suppose that's pretty well what I would say if asked why I should think I could smoke sixty cigarettes a day for fifty odd years without getting lung cancer – well, I'm only human, which would be, of course, not my excuse for the smoking, but for not expecting, or willingly accepting, the consequences. 'I'm only human,' I say to myself, and to prove to myself that I am add, 'It's not fair!'

Actually, it would be only human for the many doctors I've seen over the last six weeks to say, 'You've smoked sixty cigarettes a day for the last fifty years, and written boastfully about it! What did you expect! Everybody told you, warned you, indeed threatened you with exactly what's happening to you! Talk about serves you right! Talk about own fault! And now you come to us and you ask us to make you well again! How can we make a man well from over fifty years of sixty a day! I should hope we can't! Yes, I'm glad we can't, it would make nonsense of cause and effect, crime and punishment, if ever a man deserved to die from lung cancer, that man is standing before us now, cap in hand! Hah!' Actually, it would be fag in hand, if only I had the nerve. I've never needed cigarettes more than when getting the news that I'm dying from them.

In fact, they register my answer to the question 'Are you a smoker?' – always put in neutral – with an equally neutral smile. Not one of them has suggested, in tone or gesture, a hint of reproach. They've all been – what? The trouble is that there have been so many of them that they've concentrated themselves into a single figure, young-to-middle-aged male, spruce, in a neat suit, greeting me with gloomy courtesy, and at some point in the conversation making brief but significant physical contact – a squeeze on the shoulder, a touch on my wrist. The gloomy courtesy and the shoulder or wrist squeeze or touch I came to recognise. I think I recognised it the first time it happened, actually, as a kind of mimed proclamation of my death sentence.

# A Glimpse of My Undertaker

Sentence, yes, as I was writing the last sentence, lo! three of these doctors suddenly came into focus. One of them, the first, was Indian or Pakistani by complexion, and had a Persian-sounding name, but in every other respect he was English – his accent was what used to be called Essex, the sort of accent deployed to conceal an expensive education, which his casually sophisticated syntax and vocabulary exposed. And he knew how to pause. At one point in our third – and so far last – conversation, when all the medical evidence was in, and it was finally established that the tumour on my neck was a secondary from the tumour in my lung, he engineered one of these pauses – difficult to know how he did it, created a space in the conversation that was an actively solemn invitation to ask a question, and not simply a question, but *the* question, the only possible question – which Victoria and I resolutely refused to ask. We had agreed – no, we hadn't had to agree, it was understood between us – that the answer to this question that we weren't going to ask contained information that we didn't want to possess. So on and on and on went the pause, and then he frowned – he had a fine but undistinguished, or do I mean indistinctive, face, with an innately melancholy tinge to its dusky hue – what do I mean? How can a face have an 'innately melancholy tinge', especially when its hue is dusky? All I mean is that he somehow exuded melancholy without visibly, in the play of his features etc., expressing it. It might have been a professional acquisition, a product of his medical training, this ability to create a melancholy atmosphere simply by sitting still and smiling pleasantly, he might be equally adept at summoning up a carefree, indeed merry atmosphere without apparent effort when a different patient, with a longer future, entered his office – anyway, back to the silence, which Victoria and I were determined not to fill until he broke it himself by interpreting it for us – 'Ahem,' he said, and that's not a device on my part, he said it in two syllables – 'Ah' and then 'hem', as if 'hem' were a noun, but an abstract one. So – 'Ah-hem' (pause) 'Is there anything you perhaps want to ask me?' (little pause) 'At this time.' We didn't speak, we made negative sounds and gestures, little shakes of the head, so forth. 'Well then,' he said, getting up from behind his desk, standing there until we got up, then crossed the room and laid a hand quietly on my shoulder before moving on to open the door. As we

left the room I had the feeling that we had just con-
ferred with my undertaker.

## And on to a Party

I remember that we went home befuddled, not quite
able to speak to each other yet, perhaps not wanting
to speak about the pause and its implications, and
then realised, almost before our front door closed
behind us, that we had to go straight out again, to a
drinks party for Ian Jack, my editor at Granta, who
was retiring from the publishing side of his life. We'd
become close since he'd asked me to contribute
something to the magazine, and then encouraged me
to make a book out of it, and really, it seemed to me
that we had to go to the party. After all, I might be
dying but I wasn't actually ill, at least I didn't feel it.
So we went to a mansion in Holland Park set in magnificent grounds, with a grand and fine lawn at the
back where the party was mainly taking place. It was
a quite gorgeous evening, and of course there were
a lot of people that we knew, and of course I was
asked, in an entirely social way, how I was, and I
replied either in an entirely social way, 'Very well,
thanks, how are you?' or 'Actually, I've just been told
that I've got lung cancer, a possible secondary here,'

22

touching the lump on my neck. I don't know why I did this, or what my selection principle was, if there was one. I think it must have been that to people I knew very well, friends, I gave the second answer, and to people I only meet on this kind of occasion, I gave the sociable answer, but it might easily have been the other way around, I was in such a muddle of thoughts and feelings at the time, and it's still all a bit of a muddle now. I have an idea, though, I'd half decided that it was better to come out with the news and get it over with, also that if I told a few people I wouldn't have to go on telling people, word would get around, it always does – though there's the chance, I suppose, that at a party where there was champagne and fine wine and publishing and literary gossip in the air, as well as possibly other stuff, like romance, sex, jealousy, envy – who knows what goes on at literary parties? So who knows whether my news was taken in, or held on to long enough to get passed on? Perhaps it would be dimly remembered by some the next day, but would they get the right illness? Yes, yes, they would, the word cancer always sticks, but then would they get the right victim, would they remember the cancer but fish for a name to go with it? Well, the problem didn't occur to me then, and now it seems less a problem than a comic possibility – people in the pink of health being greeted with compassionate smiles and averted eyes, or even avoided altogether – there are people who tend to avoid the ill, not out of hardness of heart or fear of contamination, but out of embarrassment – not knowing what to say, what attitude to take.

Well, as I say, I have no idea who I told, and what confusions I may have caused, I have so little clear memory of particular moments, though there were a few people who came up to me, knowing me to be a smoker, and asked for a cigarette, although I wasn't smoking myself, for once I didn't want a cigarette – I refrained from saying as I held out the packet and then lit their cigarette, 'Oh, by the way, that reminds me, I've got lung cancer.'

Looking back on the party now, I see it as if it were a painting, all those people on the great lawn in the dying light of a soft summer evening, it's a lovely picture, although, unlike the Doge of Venice, I can't see myself in it.

## A Patriarch Calls

It's one thing to go about at a party, telling people in a slapdash sort of way that you've got lung cancer, quite another to tell the people who have a right to know, and to do so with due care and attention. 'I must tell my children,' I said to Victoria. Normally I would have named them, as in, 'I must tell Ben and Lucy that my email is down/that we're going away for a week,' whatever. They're both parents themselves after all, and have provided me with four magnificent grandchildren – from Ben two boys, Josh and Louis, both into their teens, in fact Josh almost out of them; and from Lucy two girls, Madeleine into her teens, Georgina on the fringe. Nevertheless, 'my children' seemed the appropriate phrase for the circumstances. It embraced them all, children and grandchildren, with the suggestion of generations to come. It was patriarchal. Biblical. I remember reminding myself before I phoned, Ben first and Lucy immediately after – I think, in accordance with seniority – that I must be honest without being worrying. They have worries enough of their own – who doesn't?

Lucy has a warm, chuckly voice, a delight to listen to, even when she's vexed, which isn't often, while Ben has many voices, which he uses for many effects, some of them comic, even when he's vexed, which is quite often. My dead brother Piers, Ben's uncle, was also a gifted mimic. I hear his voice in Ben's when he's imitating a policeman, for instance, but never when he's just being himself.

Talking to the children on the phone, especially consecutively, often provides almost opposite experiences, Lucy a calm one, Ben a tumultuous one, but on this occasion they were remarkably similar. I tried to keep my own voice at the casual murmur they know so well, but I could hear that it was hoarse, and possibly too low. They had to keep saying, 'What? What did you say, Dad?' and asking me to speak up. I got through all the medical stuff fluently enough – tumour here, tumour there, both small, etc. – mentioned radiotherapy and chemotherapy as likely treatments, and was able to say, when asked stumblingly what was the prognosis, that there hadn't been one, absolutely not, and didn't add, 'And there won't be, not if I can help it.'

As I muttered gutturally on they relaxed into a sort of parental sympathy, offering advice about diet and exercise, and when I said, 'And you know, when you get to my sort of age, these things happen,' neither of them said, 'Especially if you smoke, Dad.' And both said, 'But you're not old Dad, not really!', which was soothing, with a bit of a twinge in it, because I now suspect that 'old' isn't just how far you are from the beginning, but how close you are to the end.

At the earliest possible point I switched the subject – always a good tactic if you do it abruptly enough – and eventually the conversations became almost routine, the one with Ben ending in jokes and laughter, the one with Lucy in her having to hang up, it was time to collect the girls from school.

So. So I had told my children, and was quite light-headed with relief. I remember wondering though about Maddie and Gee-Gee, who were coming to lunch on a Sunday soon. Would they be told in their turn – yea, unto the next generation? – and if so what would they feel about having a cancerous Granddaddy? Would I see it in their eyes, their expressions, the way they talked to me?

## Doctor Number Two: Mummy's Delight

The second doctor, who came after the Persian-named doctor, had a Welsh name but was a magnificent-looking specimen of Anglo-Saxon manhood, though not of his own generation. He might have been an admired young friend of my parents, say ten years younger than they were when they were in their middle years. Mummy would have adored him, he was so shy and yet so easy in his manner, and his eyes had the right amount of exhaustion in them, as if he'd just come off duty – an arduous round in the hospital ward after a long morning at the operating table, nev-

ertheless, nevertheless here he was, at our service, full
of mumblingly decent apologies for having kept us
waiting, half guessing that we'd noticed the way his
eyes had avoided ours as he'd crossed the otherwise
empty waiting room, his face lowered urgently into
his mobile on his way to his office. So we waited there
for half an hour before he sent for us. You could tell
that he had colleagues to consult, patients to respond
to, almost certainly a young wife and two or three
small ones, and who knows what other obligations
clamouring for his attention. He was slightly sloppy
in that old-fashioned public school sort of way, his
youthfully grey hair flopped down over his eye and
his tie flopped out of his jacket and yet so much of
him so slightly awry and askew somehow con-
tributed to the effect of great competence – an ama-
teur in private life, needing to be mothered and
pampered and teased by his girlfriends, but a professional in his profession, magisterial with a scalpel and
forceps, effortlessly masterful with the nurses.

This is all guesswork and possibly nonsense. I've
no idea what he's really like, I know nothing about
him except that I didn't like him, and that's probably relevant information about me and not about
him, my reaction to his causing me physical distress
and what came after it.

He made me sit on a stool in the corner of his

office and tilt my head back and then he threaded through one of my nostrils a stiff wire with a camera at the end, and then wiggled and jiggled it down my throat. As he did this he explained that he was look-ing for signs of cancer in my tonsils and such places. Well, of course I hated him while he was doing it, it was worse than painful, one's nostrils and throat belong so completely to oneself – and he'd given no warning – just asked me to sit on the stool, tilt my head back and then performed the other-end-of-the-body version of a colonoscopy, and it was almost, though of course not quite – nothing could be – as foul an invasion of one's most tender and childish self – but I didn't go on hating him after he'd done it, or even disliking him. Why I disliked him then, and still do now, was that as he put the instrument away, he said, 'Well, there's nothing bad, nothing cancerous going on down there, which is reassur-ing.' A lie, you see. Not, I mean, that there was 'noth-ing bad, nothing cancerous going on down there' – doubtless true, apart from the rawness and bruising occasioned by himself – the lie was in his pretend-ing that this was 'reassuring'. I wanted, indeed des-perately hoped, that something bad was indeed going on down there. It would have meant that I had an independent cancer that would explain the tumour in my neck. With cancer two is better than one, two tumours from two separate cancers can be operated on separately, and separately eliminated. However, if the two tumours are from one cancer, they can't be operated on at all. If the tumour in the neck is from the tumour in the lung, the cancer cells are in the blood therefore, and nothing can be done. I knew all this because the first doctor, with the Persian-sounding name – let me call him Omar from now on – had not only explained it to me but in fact sent me to the present doctor precisely in the hope that he would find something cancerous going on.

But this Welsh-named doctor, let's call him Morgan Morgan and be done with it, thought – well, what did he think? Oh, I suppose only that he could delude us into thinking that bad news was good news – after all, it sounded like good news – no sign of cancer down there, rejoice! whoopee! – then he could avoid the sort of conversation that would follow giving the bad news as bad news – 'I'm very sorry, no sign of a cancer there, you're a dead man' – that sort of conversation. We didn't quite have that sort of conversation, though in fact I let him know that I understood the real significance of what he'd said. 'But we wanted to find cancer there, didn't we, surely?' I asked, not tremblingly, quite calmly. For a moment he faltered, skidded so to speak into his mumbling shyness, punctuated by apologetic laughs and abstracted hand gestures, then got himself into the clear by refusing to find his own findings conclusive – 'You never know what's there until you've had a proper look. The best thing is for me to operate. Then we'll know for sure' – and then on to suggesting dates and so forth. 'The sooner we know for sure, the quicker we can get on with it.' Getting on with it being – what exactly is the 'it' we'd be getting on with? 'Ah. That will depend on what we find.' The pause that followed wasn't engi-neered by him Omar-style. He wanted it as little as we did, and when he ended it with, 'Now, if there's anything you'd like to ask me?' he wasn't inviting a question, he was finishing the meeting, he was ris-ing from his desk, he was opening the door, and the brush of his hand on my shoulder, while not exactly a push, made me feel that I was being gently encour-aged out of his sphere of attention. To Victoria he gave his hand, tentatively, with a mumbling of soft farewells, and the sweetest of smiles. Yes, Mummy would have adored him. Morgan Morgan knows his onions when it comes to women, 'a bit of a lady's man, my dear, such a charming manner!'

And such a charming glimpse I suddenly had of his ruin, headlines in the *Daily Mail*, with a photo of Mr Floppy Morgan Morgan on his way to court, and inset, photos of the women he'd betrayed, some of

them while under anaesthetic – all of them now emotionally dead, or dying, or at the very least in tatters
as a consequence of his favourite lie – 'Oh no, don't
you worry, child, nothing bad going on down there
– that's the reassuring thing about me, you know,
the good news about me, look you, that nothing bad
ever goes on down there – married? children? who
told you that? It's a bloody untruth, you know, look
you!'

## An Ideal Passenger

We've already settled in to being here. This morning
Victoria hired a car and we went for a short spin –
first along the coast road and then into town, Agios
Nikolaus, which looked extremely lively, not only a
tourist town but a town in its own right, part of it
built around a harbour, and another part built
around a lake, but we couldn't investigate it properly because we couldn't find anywhere to park, the
one-way system is immensely confusing, so that we
kept turning down streets that we then had to back
out of, we really had to do some very skilful
manoeuvring, and put up with impatient honking
and unnecessarily aggressive gestures. Under the
circumstances, in the bedlam of a busy Greek town,

we remained remarkably calm, imperturbable. I say 'we' in this grand way because, though I don't actually drive, I take on my share of the responsibility. I sit in the passenger seat, staring out of the window and exclaiming on matters of interest – 'Hey, look at that couple over there! They must be Brits! Scots I'll bet. Only the Scots could wear shorts like that, with legs like that, both of them, and their tattoos, what's his say, on his arm?' And, 'Hey, there's a shop that sells English newspapers, and I can see the *Herald Tribune*, I wonder if they get the *Spectator*, why don't you pull over?' In other words I do my best to keep her entertained, and never let her glimpse my impatience and frustration at her inability to follow my impulses and commands.

After we'd found ourselves going down the same street for the third time, we decided to go back to the hotel and swim. We've already had a lot of swims – we start off by going down to the beach before breakfast. Victoria used never to do this, and I suspect that she's only doing it now because she's not sure how my strength will hold, and wants to keep an eye on me, if she can't see me she'll worry about me – a version of what I feel in London, when it's time to walk the dogs at night and I hate the thought of going out, but hate the thought of her going out on her own even more, knowing that every minute she's gone I'll worry that some London foulness, a twelve-year-old with a knife or a rampaging police car, will befall her. Of course, once we're out on the pavement I'm pleased I've come, although I can't say I love doing it as much as Victoria now loves our early-morning swims. We're usually the only people on the beach, and always the only people in the water, which is actually warmer at that hour than later in the day. Or is that an illusion, to do with body heat and so forth? This morning it was so still and warm and clear that after we'd got out and dried ourselves we found ourselves going back in again, without really intending to. I wish there were a way of just dissolving in the sea, without having to go through the business of drowning first.

## Unclean! Unclean!

We spent the three weeks before the operation in Suffolk, during the only part of the summer that was like summer. It was beautiful, fresh and green and yet warm, and the light soft, like a dream, really, a dream of England that only the previous months of bad weather could have given us. We walked every evening for an hour or so, swam in the mornings and sometimes the afternoons in a friend's swimming pool, and at night – at night –

At night I tried to write but couldn't, because, well, what was the point? And I tried to stop smoking, but again, well, what was the point? Nevertheless, I cut down to about fifteen a day, and felt proud of myself.

I read familiar things that comforted me, mainly Wordsworth, Edward Thomas, Hardy, and Larkin's essays, and sometimes I sat in the garden in the moonlight, or as the dawn came up. There is no silence like a Suffolk night, in my experience, until the birds come, to shred your nerves. One night I sat for a long time at my desk in my study without doing anything at all until I suddenly began to beat myself about the head, I think in an attempt to make myself cry. I know I quite often wanted to cry, as if crying would bring release, but release from what? There was nothing to be released from. I wasn't in any pain. In fact I hadn't felt so well, physically, for a long time, not for a couple of years. Knowledge, perhaps. Yes, it must have been knowledge that I wanted to be released from.

About a week before the operation, we were still in Suffolk, my mobile rang, and a pleasant voice, female, middle-aged, practical, asked me if I was Mr Simon Gray. I said I was. 'Oh, good,' she said, and asked me if I knew that I'd got – I couldn't make out at first what it was that she wanted to know if I knew I'd got, it didn't actually seem to be a word, or a group of words – actually it turned out to be a group of letters, which she translated for me as methicillin-resistant *Staphylococcus aureus* bacteria, otherwise known as the infamous MRSA. 'What do you mean?' I said. 'I've got MRSA! How can I have got MRSA? You get it from hospitals, don't you? And the only hospital I've been to is yours.' She explained that I hadn't got it in the hospital, I'd brought it in with me, they'd found it when they'd taken a swab from one of my nostrils. I suddenly recalled having a nostril swabbed, done so swiftly and matter-of-factly that I'd scarcely registered it. 'How disgusting!' I said. 'I'm sorry, I had no idea, no idea –' 'Oh, it's quite all right, Mr Gray,' she said very pleasantly. 'About 50 per cent of the people in this country have MRSA. It doesn't do them or anyone else any harm, except when they come into a hospital. But it never comes into our hospital. We make sure of that. That's why we swab you. But you'll have to get rid of it before your operation.' Then she told me to surrender myself, so to speak, to a local doctor, she would email to him or her the necessary information, and then I was to follow the following instructions: I was to shampoo my body, with particular attention to my armpits, my chest, and between my legs three times a day; gargle three times a day; take antibiotics three times a day; if I performed these things for five consecutive days, the MRSA would be gone by the date of my operation. The gargle, the shampoo and the antibiotics would be prescribed by the doctor, and would be available from any chemist. If by any chance I forgot the instructions, the doctor and the chemist would be able to remind me of them. Was that all right, Mr Gray? I said it was. 'Then we'll see you for your operation as scheduled.' She added, 'And don't worry. It's all quite usual, Mr Gray.' When I thought about the conversation afterwards I felt there was something slightly odd about it, not simply the subject, but her manner, her tone, what was it? And eventually I realised it was the way she'd addressed me, not only formally, as Mr Gray, but regularly, slipping it into almost every sentence. I remembered that on my first visit to the hospital I'd been asked whether I wanted to be called by my first name or as Mr, and I'd said 'Mr'. Her using it so often in such a brief conversation on such a subject could have seemed satirical, but in fact it had been calming, positively soothing. I'd really felt almost dignified when confirming that I understood what I must do to render my body hygienic, and to prevent it from being a source of possibly fatal sickness to others. I wondered if she'd been trained in

tact, or came by it naturally. Either way, I was grateful, and reminded myself of it as I applied the obnox-
iously powerful shampoo to my pubic hair and
gargled with the vile pinkish mouthwash, and so
kept at bay certain scenes from films, I think
American prison films of the 1940s, when the con-
victs are forced to de-louse themselves, whether they
have lice or not, as part of a humiliation ritual –

The operation was scheduled –

but I mustn't forget the local doctor, who gave me
the prescriptions for the shampoo, mouthwash and
antibiotics. He has his practice, with which Victoria
had had dealings since she had first come to Suffolk,
in an old and elegant house in the nearby market
town. His office looks out on the main square, it's a
large and civilised room, and the swish modern
computer on the handsome and antiquey desk is at
odds with it, but his hands played skilfully over its
keyboard as he brought up the details sent from the
London hospital. He was a slight man, very young
by my standards, somewhere in his late forties, I'd
guess, and mildly elegant, in a countrified sort of
way, with a shy manner of speaking, and a trace of a
Suffolk accent. He looked at the screen for a while,
then turned and let his gaze settle between Victoria
and myself, sitting in nice chairs, facing him. 'You
have cancer?' 'Yes,' I said. 'In the lung?' 'Yes,' I said,

and added, 'And possibly the neck. Though it might be a secondary.' 'Yes,' he said. 'You see, I had to ask, before I could write the prescription.' There was a little pause, and his eyes came towards me, shyly. 'I'm sorry,' he said. 'I'm very sorry.' I couldn't really think of anything to say. I was touched, of course, because it was so feelingly said, but also shocked, because it was so feelingly said. I'd got into the habit, during our time in the country, of thinking of my illness as a secret. Well, not exactly a secret but as belonging to another aspect of my life, not shared with anyone but Victoria and the people in the hospital in London. In the last few days I'd even found, not a serenity exactly, certainly not at night, alone in my garden study, but during the day, during our walks and after them – they were such perfectly beautiful days, long and tender and bright days – and now in the doctor's office a decent and kindly young man had, without intending to, unravelled me, and there was the disbelief, the inner gaping at the impossible, as of hearing the news for the first time. 'Is there anything else I can do?' he asked, as he handed me the prescription. 'Are you all right for – well, sleeping, anxiety, depression – that sort of thing, what are you taking for them?' I couldn't remember, but Victoria could. 'Well, that sounds all right. If you run out of anything just give me a ring.'

We walked across the square to the chemist, where we got the shampoo, mouthwash and antibiotics. The town looked old in the evening, old and well used, and the hotel where Dickens and Mr Pickwick had stayed – sometimes you look at familiar places as if you've never seen them before, or will never see them again – perhaps it's the same sort of look.

## Incriminating Evidence

The day before the operation I had to go in and be tested, to make sure that the shampoo, the mouthwash and the antibiotics had cleaned the MRSA out of me. We were very nearly late, as the traffic was appalling, and then the road beside the hospital, where we park, was blocked off for cars for the usual London reasons, so I got out and hurried down it, having arranged to meet Victoria at the pub where we always went after one of my appointments – in fact I passed the pub on my way down the street, and had a momentary jolt when I saw a man sitting at one of the tables on the pavement – he looked very like one of the doctors that I had routine dealings with until the cancer made him irrelevant – a short, very handsome Yorkshireman, with a lopsided smile, bright blue eyes and a wry, charming manner

– let me call him Dr Mumby – Victoria thought Dr Mumby very attractive and I liked him too – when he was warning me about my smoking, he would do it in a murmuring, shoulder-shrugging sort of way, sympathetic – his father was a chain-smoker, he said, so he knew how difficult it was to give up, and to get people to give up, this with a smile to Victoria and a nod at me – well, the man sitting outside the pub, talking intensely to a middle-aged woman in a white coat, looked, as I've said, very like this doctor, so like in fact that I couldn't understand how I knew it wasn't until I realised that he was smoking, indeed he was talking around his cigarette in a very prac-tised manner, almost like a gangster in an old movie, so I didn't shout a greeting as I went past, and when I looked back just before I went in, I could see clearly that it wasn't Dr Mumby, it wasn't just the cigarette that looked gangsterish, but the whole of him, his posture, his clothes, the cut of his jib.

All the test amounted to was a swab-taking, and there was something else, I think, I can't remember, but I didn't have to wait, it was done, the swab and whatever else they did to me, within minutes of my arrival, and then I had to wait a while, sitting on a hard chair in the corridor, for the result. I don't think that took long, but I felt very tense, as if waiting to hear whether I was rid of a sexually transmitted disease. A nurse came and told me that I was OK – I don't remember what she looked like because I avoided looking at her, I didn't want her to see the relief on my face. I went out, and there was Victoria, I could see her sitting at the table next to the one at which the pseudo-Mumby had sat. 'It's fine,' I said as I approached her. 'No more MRSA,' or words to that effect. 'Good,' she said. 'Guess who was here a moment ago, he's just left.' 'No,' I said. 'It wasn't Dr Mumby. He was smoking.' 'Yes, it was Dr Mumby,' she said. 'He recognised me. And he wasn't smoking. At least –' she got up and together we looked under his table. There was a cigarette end, half smouldering. 'Well well,' we said. 'Well well well.' Victoria looked quite pleased, probably because the thought of him furtively dropping the cigarette under the table on spotting the wife of a chain-smoking patient made him seem engagingly naughty and boyish, and I felt pleased too, though I don't quite know why.

## I Sense an Opportunity for Self-improvement

The operation was scheduled for 1.30 p.m., no food or water for eight hours before. I had a little room at the end of a ward, a sombre little room, no doubt clean in fact but grubby in atmosphere, with a history of death, or so I felt as I stood by the bed holding my overnight bag, which contained pyjamas, toothbrush, books, writing pad and pens. 'Yes, it has a history of death,' I said to Victoria, nodding to the walls as if I could see on them the outlines of dreadful stains, and nodding to the bed and the ghostly line of corpses that lay on it, and then nodding around the room as a whole, at the memory of all the grieving relatives – or no grieving relatives, just the necessary functionaries cleaning and folding up the bodies of men and women of my sort of age who'd arrived clutching their overnight bags –

It was a miserable business, lying on the high, narrow bed waiting for an operation that was postponed, and again postponed, and then again postponed, becoming light-headed from hunger and dehydration. By the time I got to the knife I'd been without food and water for thirteen hours, no time at all, I realise, for the many heroes and victims that pass through all kinds of epic ordeals in war zones, no time at all for the many elderly NHS patients abandoned on trolleys in hospital corridors, forgotten, unnoticed, unfed, unwatered, unchanged, lying in their own excrement and urine, some for days on end, 'here – here and in England' – but for me, pampered as I've always been by circumstances and by the love, care and attention of others, this short period of deprivation, during which I could at least keep myself clean, was – well, it was a miserable business – made worse by my absolute conviction that Morgan Morgan had seen as much as he needed to see when he pushed his camera down my throat by way of the wire he threaded through my nostril – further gouging about with scalpels and such would tell him only what he already knew, and that I knew he knew – for him the consolation for the waste of effort would be a fee, for me that I'd been taught a lesson, a lesson in patience, humility, fortitude, all departments of the moral life in which I'm weak – if I hope to get up to the required standard in the time left to me, I shall have to do some cramming, so start by being grateful to Dr Morgan Morgan for bringing you to that forlorn little room, and letting you linger there, in hunger and thirst –

## His Spurs and Trousers, My Shoes – A Digression

Like any good and happily married man, I share my sufferings, as much as I can, with my wife. There's not much Victoria can do about the sheer blank terror and disbelief – the self alone with the self – so she does all the things I can't, for lack of will and morale, do myself – fixing and remembering all the appointments, packing up the overnight bag, organising the taxi, getting me to the right hospital entrance, to the right admissions desk, to the right ward. I sometimes wonder if she had all these skills before I entered her life, or has she had to acquire them as we went along? She does it all with such consideration, tact, kindness and grace – such charm and softness and delicacy – all these on my account, for me. And in return she has a bewildered, angry, blustering, ungrateful – yes, frequently ungrateful – shameful to write it down, how ungrateful I've been, am being, for all that she gives me that helps me get through all the things I have to get through in order to get to the end, the only end of all this.

And when I get there, have got there, am gone, what will it be like for her? Going into my study, for instance. Well, I should think it'll be quite – quite – I can't imagine it. I suppose I mean that I don't want to imagine it –

Well then, what about others, people who know me but have never seen my study? What will they make of it? Can I imagine that? Well, I have experience to draw on. For instance, when I visited Ian's flat after his death, because I was told that he wanted me to have something, a book or a print – in fact, I took his straw hat, which he'd worn to cover his balding and blotched head during chemo – I was moved by the atmosphere of dedication as well as of loneliness. He'd moved into it as a halfway house between his marriage with Ahdaf and their two sons, and his intended marriage to Patchy, by whom he had two young children, a daughter and a son. It didn't look like the flat of a man who'd ever lived with anyone else, it was neat and organised in a bachelor's way. Most striking were the number of television sets, all with fairly up-to-date systems, and recording devices – one in every room, and in one room two sets – can that be right? – so that he would never miss a football match, whichever room he was in. He watched virtually every match shown on television, he told me, which even five years ago was an enormous number, but then football was his passion. Well, Tottenham Hotspur, Spurs, was his passion and football in general the context in which his passion flourished and smouldered. I remember once he wanted to change the evening for a dinner because Spurs were playing Newcastle in a cup tie but for reasons I can't remember I was determined to keep him to the arrangement. I told him I would record the match, then after dinner – we always met at Chez Moi, a little restaurant almost opposite our house – we'd watch it in my study. He felt anxious about this, was sure something would go wrong, but I said I'd recorded hundreds of matches, it wouldn't go wrong, why should it? So he agreed, slightly mutteringly, that that's what we'd do. I set the video timer just before crossing the road to Chez Moi, then, to make sure all was well, I recorded something, I don't remember what, and played it back. The screen filled with white dots on a blank background. I tried to phone Ian to tell him not to come, to stay at home and watch the match. I was too late. He'd already left and I got the answering machine. I almost panicked, then had a moment of inspiration – I phoned Philip, who has a car hire firm and has taken us, Victoria and me, to airports and first nights and special occasions for many years now and has become a friend who furthermore often records things for us when we're away. He promised to tape the match and as soon as it was finished to bring it to the restaurant. I crossed the road to Chez Moi and found Ian already ensconced. He listened with suspicion as I explained what had happened, and what I'd arranged to rectify it, and when I'd finished he looked uneasy and impatient. 'It'll be all right,' I said. 'Philip never lets me down, he'll be here with the tape as promised, we'll see every moment of the match.' He shook his head and muttered that the

47

evening was beginning to have a smell of calamity. He was probably on the verge of taxiing back to his flat and watching what was left – he'd get most of the second half – but he didn't. He got through the meal restlessly, constantly checking his watch and then, pretty well the minute he judged the match to be over, eyeing the door and saying things like, 'Where is this Philip of yours?' – and I kept saying things like, 'Give him a chance, he lives twenty minutes away.' In fact, he turned up with the tape before we'd finished our coffee, and said that he'd tested it to make sure it had come through clearly, and then wound it back to the beginning, it was set, ready to be played. Ian and I went back to my study, I put a drink and an ashtray beside him, turned on the television, put in the tape, sat down, got up again as Ian groaned aloud, the groan of a man who'd known all along that there was no hope. The screen was black, with white dots. Instead of cursing Philip, in whom I had complete faith, I sauntered in a confident manner to the video, checked that the tape was in properly, checked that the set was on the right channel, pressed a few buttons at random and suddenly there it was on the screen, a perfect picture, the sound also perfect. Ian lit a cigarette and settled tensely in his chair. I sat watching from my desk, also smoking and at first offering observations and bits of analysis until I realised from his answering grunts and silences that they weren't wanted, indeed that he found them irritating because they interfered with his concentration. So it was in full, uninterrupted concentration that he watched Newcastle score one, then two, then three, then four, then five goals. Spurs scored none. When the match was over, frowning commentators discussed whether Spurs had finally reached rock bottom. Before they'd finished Ian got up. I walked him to Holland Park Avenue, where he hailed a taxi. 'Thanks,' he said, in a dead tone as he got in. 'Thanks a lot.' I'd always thought of myself as a man who loved football and watched it avidly, but I supported the team that played the sort of football that I most enjoyed watching, and it tended to change from season to season, sometimes within the season. That evening with Ian made it clear that there was a world of difference between a man who followed the game and a man who followed a club. In Ian's eyes, I realised, I was little more than a dilettante, while he was a man who had given his heart and his loyalty to Spurs, who had just been beaten 5–0, and had hit rock bottom.

It wasn't a surprise, then, to find so many television sets in his flat, but it was poignant to see them there, so tactically arranged. It gave one a glimpse into his habits, with the piercing thought that he'd never turn them on again, just as he'd never sit at his desk again. There were papers spread on it, a couple of open books. And then there was his bedroom, with a single bed, neatly made, the whole room, the whole flat was neat, have I already said that? neat and orderly, so unlike his emotional and financial life. Over the chair in his bedroom was draped a pair of trousers, looking as if they were waiting for him to get into them.

But to get back to my own case, my study after my death, what would people see? Well, there are the books chaotically everywhere, the desk with my typewriter on it and some papers, the other desk with my computer and probably some yellow pads full of illegible writing, the portraits on the wall, Schubert and Dickens, a couple of cricketers by Spy, a lovely watercolour of a frog, done by the father of a good friend. All in all, pretty well what you'd expect of a man who does the sort of things I did, but oh yes, except for the shoes, of course, all my shoes lined up against the wall of my study – I've just counted them in my head, got up to twelve pairs, most of them worn only once or twice as they'd changed size the moment after I'd bought them, others that I've used for over twenty years, and somehow look as if my feet are still in them even when they're empty, and there are the espadrilles with holes in the toes and flattened-down heels, and there's a round box with more shoes in them, sneakers and trainers and sandals, and up in the bedroom closet a couple of pairs of shiny black shoes, for smart occasions, they pinch and squeeze my feet and I only put them on if I know I'll be able to sit down for most of the evening, or best of all kick them off under the dinner table –

What will it be like for her, all those shoes to deal with, with all of them, even the unworn ones, having a sort of history to them? I wonder if I shouldn't start getting rid of them when we get back, a pair or so at a time, so that Victoria won't notice. But where would I take them? Oxfam? Put them in carrier bags and taxi them up to Oxfam, say two bags a week. But supposing she went into Oxfam, as she does sometimes, and saw all the shoes lined up against the wall there – what would she think? what would it mean, that I'd been secretly disposing of my shoes? But why secretly? Surely I could say, 'Darling, don't you think it's time –' No. Stop there. You couldn't say that. So let's move on from shoes to ties, because a) I've only got three or four of them and b) I never wear them anyway.

# A Visit from Mummy's Delight

I woke from the operation some time after midnight with a bursting bladder. It took me several minutes to get out of bed and into the bathroom, where I discovered that my bladder wouldn't empty, and nor would my bowels. Both were becoming painful. I passed this information on to a nurse, who passed it on to a mortifyingly pretty doctor (female), who came in with a gadget that I recognised from some ten years ago, after an operation on my stomach had left me with the problems that I now had again. She was deft, as well as pretty, the doctor. She had curly black hair, an olive complexion, alert brown eyes and a mouth that would have looked even more delightful if she'd allowed it to smile. It took her about three minutes to insert my penis into the catheter, or is it technically the other way round, and I only screamed once, though at length. She went out and returned immediately with a nurse, who hitched me up to a drip. So there I was for the night – the tube of a catheter in my penis, my right hand attached to a drip, my throat – my throat was in waiting, underneath the painkillers. The next morning, shortly after Victoria arrived with newspapers, an oddly shifty little nurse, I took her to be, poked her head around the door and said something so incomprehensible that I knew it must be English. I looked to Victoria to translate and, when she couldn't, asked the nurse if she'd mind – I hadn't quite understood. This time she spoke slowly and clearly, if rather nervously.

'Dr Morgan Morgan is doing his rounds and would like to visit you if you have no objections.'

I said of course I had no objections, was indeed anxious to have a few words with Dr Morgan Morgan.

'That's very kind of you,' she said, and withdrew.

'How strange,' we thought, that the doctor who'd operated on me should seek permission to speak to me. Or perhaps he'd been informed of my catheter-bruised penis, my drip-tube imprisoned arm, my swollen bowels, and felt responsible for them, as indeed he was, although only accidentally, at least I assumed accidentally.

Morgan Morgan came in a few minutes after the shifty little nurse-figure had withdrawn, and he came in accompanied by the shifty little nurse-figure, who I now realised was actually a shifty little doctor-figure, a junior doctor or trainee doctor, as were the eight or nine young men and women who stood there with her, all of them looking shifty – at least in relation to me, none of them able to meet my eye. Of course, what the shifty little doctor-figure had really been asking was whether Morgan Morgan could bring in his students and display me to them, for educational purposes. I didn't feel humiliated so much as humbled – brought low – an object of study and later of discussion. Morgan Morgan stood in the middle of his semicircle and wondered how I was. I said I was fine, really, under the circumstances, apart from a sore throat and – I gestured with my un-attached hand towards my attached one, but decided not to mention the catheter. 'Well,' he said, seemingly at a loss, 'that's good. And – well – we didn't find anything bad in your throat, except a slightly septic tonsil, which I took out. But that was all. Nothing wrong down there, no cancer is the good news.' Yes, there he was, doing it again – deliv-ering unbearably bad news as if it were good news – I almost expected him, wanted him even, to say, 'Look you,' as in my caricaturing impersonations of him. Of course I hadn't been foolish enough to har-bour a hope, though hope, as we all know at bitter times in our lives, is an eager ally of foolishness, and the truth is that I had now and again, before the operation and in the uncomfortable hours since, found myself daring to harbour – such an odd phrase, to harbour a hope, as if hope drifts about in search of a haven, a resting place –

54

There were all those students' eyes that couldn't look at me.

'I thought,' I said, 'that the good news would be if you found cancer.'

He gave me a confused smile, as if I were being too clever for him.

'Your not finding cancer in my throat means that the cancer on my neck is a secondary from the cancer in my lung.'

'Well, yes,' he agreed, 'there is that.' He tried to think of something else to say. 'Thank you,' he said, 'for letting us come in to see you.' He went out, his students trailing after him, one or two of them achieving nice, apologetic smiles – apologies on behalf of youth and health to age and illness.

Victoria and I sat for a while. We didn't have much to say to each other. I thought it was odd, though, that Morgan Morgan hadn't examined me or questioned me, apart from asking me how I felt. What exactly had he been showing his junior doctors or trainees or whatever they were? What was there to see except a seventy-year-old man in a bed on a drip? They couldn't see the catheter, and wouldn't have needed to anyway, as they surely knew what a catheter was and did. From where they stood they couldn't have seen the tumour on my neck, so what was it he was showing them? Why did he want them to look at me? Unless, of course, I was his straight man in a little demonstration, or skit even, on how to dress dreadful news up as its opposite. On the other hand, perhaps there was a complicated lecture, part of which he gave before they came in, the other part after they'd gone out – 'I want you particularly to note the distinctive shape of the nose, characteristic of the heavy smoker destined for lung cancer' and then 'Which one of you would care to make an observation about the relationship between the smallness of his eyes, the lowness of his brow, and the probable sites of his third, fourth, fifth and sixth tumours?'

## Literary Wheeling and Dealing – No Wonder There's a Smell!

The next morning a nurse called Anita told me I could go home. She was a rather stern-looking woman of about forty-five, and was from Barbados. She had tended to me – emptied my urine out of the flask, adjusted the position of the drip needle in the back of my hand, taken my temperature and blood pressure etc. – in a solemn and unforgiving manner. I felt uneasy every time she came into the room, she confirmed my sense that I was there in foul circumstances – catheter, drip, tumours – because I deserved to be. When she told me that she was now going to take out the drip and the catheter tube, she made me feel that these unsavoury duties were forced upon her as the consequence of my unsavoury behaviour – and of course she was right, if you trace the thought far enough back. If I hadn't smoked I wouldn't have cancer, wouldn't have had a throat operation, wouldn't have required a drip and a catheter, neither of us would be where we now were, me in a hospital bed, she at the foot of it, staring at me. 'Are you still writing?' she asked. For a moment I wondered whether one of us had made a mistake, that either she'd said or I'd heard 'writing' instead of 'smoking', but then I noticed that her expression, though as serious as usual, was also interested, possibly even self-interested. So I said yes, I still wrote, though not much at the moment.

'I write,' she said. 'I am a writer too.'

I was very pleased to hear this. I wanted the person who was going to take the catheter tube out of my penis to want something from me, and I could sense that Anita wanted something. I couldn't wait to promise it to her, whatever it was.

'What have you written?' I asked eagerly.

It was a novel about herself and her adventures. She'd had an adventurous life, she said, strange

57

things had happened to her since her escape from Barbados.

'You escaped from Barbados?'

'I thought I would call it *Dangerous Escape*, or *My Dangerous Escape*.'

'"My" is better,' I said. 'It makes it more personal.'

'*My Dangerous Escape*.' She seemed to like the sound of it. She said it several times more, lengthening it slightly: '*My Dan – ge – rous Es – cape*.'

'What were you escaping from?' I asked. For me Barbados was one of the places I escaped to, and never wanted to leave.

'From Barbados,' she said.

Well, I suppose if you were born there, with the prospect of spending the rest of your life there, you might come to feel that you were on too little land in far too much water – and then there would be the family – parents, brothers and sisters, cousins, aunts, uncles – and the church – there are lots of churches of so many denominations that it would be hard not to belong to one of them, yes, a God-fearing people, a neighbour-fearing people, too, probably – so a perfect place for clapped-outs like me, who yearned for the England of the 1950s, but for Anita when she'd been young it might have seemed like a prison.

'Well, I suppose it's all in the book,' I said. 'Why you wanted to escape.'

She said it was. Along with all the things that had happened to her since. She'd had a difficult and exciting life, the escape from Barbados to Canada, and then from Canada to London. She had a son growing up and had a husband somewhere. She also had a good friend, a clever woman younger than herself who had advised her to write the book, and had helped her in the revising of it. Her friend thought that there was still a little work to be done on it, and then it would be ready for publication. What did I think?

I said it sounded very promising.

Yes, she said. It was. Very promising.

Her tone through all this was slightly friendlier than before, but still forbidding. I kept thinking of her fingers working the tube out of my penis, and longed to speak words that would make them gentle, coaxing, caring, loving, above all painless.

How, she asked, could she get *My Escape from Barbados* published?

I told her that it was very difficult these days to get books published, at least in my understanding of the situation. I didn't say that if she were twenty years or so younger and possibly a mite prettier – though she'd really be quite pretty, Anita, if only she'd stop frowning – actually, it was almost a scowl – so if she'd stop almost scowling – and there was a moment when she laughed, all white teeth and sparkling eyes, and her face came alive and was better than pretty – in other words I didn't tell her that her chances of getting *My Escape from Bermuda* published were minuscule unless her story included rape, alcoholism, drug addiction, racial abuse, sexual servitude.

'Best thing to do is to get an agent,' I said.

'An agent?'

'An agent will know all the publishers. She'll know which one to send your book to.'

'You have an agent?'

I said I had.

She didn't say anything, just stood there, keeping her level, authoritarian gaze fixed on me.

'Hey,' I said eventually, 'I've got an idea. Why don't I –?' and gave her my agent Judy Daish's address and several of her phone numbers, reminding myself that Judy was always superb in a crisis, and that the removal of a catheter was a crisis. Anita took a pad out of her pocket, and a pen, wrote down the address and the phone numbers, read them out to me twice, put the pen and the pad away. She didn't thank me, or smile acknowledgement, she accepted it as her due, something that I in some way owed her. I wonder, though, how she knew I was a writer.

She took the tube out in a simple, straightforward manner, very practised, but not particularly sensitively – I mean, she didn't seem either touched or irritated by my scream of pain. After this one conversation she didn't refer to *My Escape from Barbados* again, though she was in and out of my room quite often, for pulse and temperature etc., and the next day, when she came in to tell me that I could go home, and I wished her luck with the book, she said, 'Thank you,' in an indifferent and blank sort of way, closing off the subject.

While we were hanging about in the corridor, waiting for a doctor to come and sign the document that made it OK for me to leave, an exceptionally pretty Indian nurse came up to us. With a dazzling smile to Victoria, she turned to me and said in an intimate and caring voice, 'I hope you won't mind my mentioning it, but you smell of urine.' I suppose that once or twice, when I was a child, an adult had said something like that to me, and perhaps as a child I was mortified, but now, as an elderly adult in dire straits, I felt nothing except a dull curiosity. 'Are you sure?' I said. 'I can't smell anything,' and asked Victoria whether she could smell urine on me. 'I don't mean to offend you,' the nurse said. 'I was

61

worried that if you go home by bus or on the tube people will say something, and you will be embarrassed. Please don't mind my mentioning it,' and she went off gracefully, on long and shapely legs, her charming head held high. 'Do I smell of urine?' I asked Victoria again. She sniffed around me, and said that I didn't, but that she'd been aware of a strong uriney smell coming from the room opposite. Its door was open and two old men lay on beds, propped up on pillows, facing each other, asleep. They were both sallow, gaunt and bald, so similar to each other that they looked related, twins almost, though I don't expect they were.

All the stuff in the hospital – the operation, Morgan Morgan, Anita, the catheter, smelling or not smelling of urine – it's all quite trivial, really, in the grand scheme of things – even in the very small grand scheme of things which is me and the rest of my life. Why, then, do I not only remember it but insist on writing it down?

## Well, What Should I Be Writing?

Wisdom? But I have none. Consolation? But I am inconsolable. I have no faith that is – in one of the current phrases I hate so much – 'fit for purpose'. No faith that isn't 'fit for purpose' either. But do I have any sort of faith, even a small, uneasy one, not perhaps 'fit for purpose' but a helpful guide through the moment-by-moment moments that I have left to live through? Of course not. I have only the self that I've been stuck with all my life. Odd that I should think that I am an I that has a self, as if I and my self weren't identical. I certainly behave as if I were in some way double, if not actually plural, especially in the last few years when I talk to myself almost continuously when on my own, and sometimes when I'm not, and also have the sense that I'm in the audience, a commentator or a judge of a debate when the dialogue becomes quarrelsome, which it frequently does. Recently, since the news, we've spoken lamentations to ourself, 'Oh, poor Simon,' we say, or 'Poor old Si,' quite affectionately, as to a dog. Or 'You stupid bugger, stupid, stupid bugger!' Or struck myself savagely in the face, as I did that night in the garden in Suffolk, swearing at myself, 'Fuck, shit, arsehole! What a stupid, fucking arsehole!' – and though I suppose I mean, specifically, for having smoked myself to death, I also mean more generally, for being a creature that dies – thinking that the relationship between me and my mortal self was a sort of arranged marriage, the fundamental terms of which I never agreed to. Could I believe that that deceived and coerced 'I' is in fact my soul, my soul 'fastened to a dying animal/It knows not what it is' – from Yeats, surely, but I can't remember which poem, and of course he believed in the soul almost as a physical being – 'unless/Soul clap its hands and sing, and louder sing/For every tatter in its mortal dress'. But no, my self isn't my soul, there's too many of it, and it's grubby and it can't sing, it's probably what I have instead of a soul, and it's not soulful, it's helpless and angry –

Does this mean, then, that I never expected to die?

Actually, I think I'll try to come back to this question later. For now let me just say that actually it's a heavenly day –

## Pleasantries and Other Pleasures

Yes, a most heavenly day. Warm, with the mildest of breezes, the sea calm and the surrounding mountains visible, with the distinct hint, like large thoughts not yet thought, of mountains beyond them, and beyond. I'm sitting at the table, as has become my habit, with my back resting against the chapel wall. In front of me are the tables and chairs of the restaurant, and then the esplanade and the steps down to the beach. It's the sort of day that helps people to be friends, almost everyone who passes by me nods or smiles, some say a few words, the routine words – 'Isn't it lovely here!' and 'What a beautiful day,' or more personally, 'You look comfortable there in the shade.' An elderly Scotsman with a verra thick accent has just loitered to discuss the charms of the hotel, it's his first time in Greece, usually he goes to Portugal 'and such', he tries to learn the language of the country he holidays in, but he's finding Greek 'verra, verra difficult' – he's been here a week, going back on Tuesday, so he doubts that he'll master it on this visit, at least – Well, it was a nice conversation, cheerful and easy. Then he was down to the beach and a few minutes later up again with a stately, heavy-treading silver-haired wife, who continued on her way while he paused to tell me to send him a cheque, a blank cheque, any sort of cheque would do as long as it was blank. I laughed and nodded, but couldn't think what to say because I didn't understand the joke, if it was a joke. Yes, it was a joke, his countenance and the tone of his voice announced it as such, but what was its point? I'm going to go for a swim, why not?

Victoria was on the beach, lolling on a sunbed, reading. I sidled up to her, reached for her hand to lead her into the sea, but coughed before I could surprise her. That's the thing about this cough. It's not the free and easy, loose and phlegmy, and on the whole controllable cough of health. It's a tight little cough, a bit of a rasper, that comes when it chooses. It's a cancer cough, as the swelling on my neck is a cancer swelling, one the audible, the other the visible sign of my condition.

Victoria has become used to the cough. As soon as she heard it she looked up, then held out her hand – and so, though I didn't succeed in surprising her, I did nevertheless lead her into the sea, which was clear and still, with only one other couple swimming, but lots of small black fish scampering near the surface. We sported about in the shallows, as I haven't yet the courage to go out of my depth. I'm not sure of my strength, whether it won't suddenly give out, as it's started to do now and then on land, when I have to pause, stoop to recover my breath, my legs heavy and weak, my shoulders sagging. If that happens in the water I can probably roll on to my back and float. On the other hand, well, there are worse deaths, some of them in bed.

Eventually Victoria went off for a proper swim and I stayed near the shore, the water just up to my neck. If I bent my knees I had the feeling of being suspended. It was really very pleasant, hanging about in the water, watching her steady breaststroke taking her away from me until the fuzz of her hair was too far out for my liking. The familiar anxiety clutched at my heart, and, as if responding to it, she turned and headed back. We got out – a nice, easy beach to get out on to, thank God – and went to the shower, an unusual shower in that it delivers the water with such force that it hits the skin like needles, and the top of one's head is sore for a few moments afterwards. Then she returned to the sunbed and her book, and I walked to the steps, intending to come back here to the chapel. But I didn't come back here, I turned around, and without actually concealing myself from Victoria slipped back into the water without her seeing me. I think I wanted to test myself out. I did all the things I've been doing since I was five or six, underwater somersaults, spiral dives, corkscrews. I went through my repertoire grimly, as if I were auditioning, then more and more freely until suddenly, without at first being conscious of it, I was enjoying myself – splashing and sporting, diving and twirling, holding my breath underwater for quite long stretches. Then I did the more taxing stuff, the two backstrokes, the sidestroke and the crawl. The backstrokes were fine, the sidestroke OK, but the crawl wasn't right. Something was out of alignment, in the small of my back or at the base of my spine. And the fact is that although I could do all the other strokes properly, I couldn't do any of them for very long, almost as if, when it came to purposeful swimming, my body had a weak will or a short attention span – it's not that I slowed down or wore myself out, I just stopped – perhaps it was to catch my breath, perhaps my lungs had abruptly emptied. But that's all right, really, perfectly all right, because I had so much pleasure from the breath that kept me afloat – yes, think of it that way, a new way, for you, of thinking about things.

As I was writing the above a young Frenchman with a perpetual half-smile and a perpetual stubble – it's been the same length for three days now, how does he do it? – stopped by to confide that he was leaving this afternoon, he was very sad, going back home to Tours, did I know Tours? I said I did, which was a lie, and a foolish one – my plan was to stop him telling me about Tours, its history, its architecture, its restaurants, after all there would be no need for him to tell me if he thought that I already knew – but he was so astonished that I knew Tours that he wanted to know when I'd been, why, and what did I think of it? So I said, 'Oh,' I said, 'it was a long time ago, and it might have been Lourdes, come to think of it, yes, Lourdes, not Tours.' He did a polite little

French gape, eyebrows up, mouth pursed, at the thought that anyone, even an Englishman, could confuse going to Lourdes with going to Tours, but then pressed on to what he really wanted to talk about, which was his new car. He was picking it up in Paris on his way to Tours, it was an English car, a beautiful car, it was a Jaguar!

'Wow!' I said.

We beamed proudly at each other, he because of his new car, I because I come from the country that made it. Then he passed on, up the path to the hotel and – I think I can say with confidence, though of course you never know – out of my life for ever. He's not somebody I would mind meeting again, he was so friendly and pleased with everything.

## Doctor Number Three: Chipmunk of Doom

I was just about to settle back against the wall of the chapel, stop writing for a while and smoke what would be only my third cigarette of the day. Only! Only your third! Yes well but – three months ago it would have been my twenty-third, thirtieth even – no, it wouldn't, it's not midday yet, three months ago you wouldn't even have been up, so you wouldn't have smoked any cigarettes, none – I've actually managed to put the cigarette back in the pack, but in order to keep it there I've got to go on writing, and I don't really want to, as I'll almost certainly find myself writing about the third doctor, the one that came after Omar and Morgan Morgan, the one I keep putting off writing about –

He wore the same sort of clothes as Omar and Morgan Morgan, dark suit, shirt, tie, but in their cases the clothes seemed both to confer authority and to imply deference. I think I described Omar as looking like an undertaker, and though Morgan Morgan gave the impression of being dishevelled the dishevelment was in his personality, he was still in absolutely the right clothes, the clothes were right for the man and the clothes were right for the job, ergo the man was right for the job, was how it worked in the cases of both Omar and Morgan Morgan. The third doctor looked wrong in all three respects, though my first impression, physical and before thought, was that he was a chipmunk, a massive chipmunk, and then the second one, when he'd formed into a man, that he was in the wrong clothes, that they were too grown-up for him. In fact, he looked like an exuberant prep-school boy, circa the period I went to prep school. His eyes popped boisterously behind the lenses of large spectacles, his straw-coloured hair stood straight up from his head as if in jubilation, and his round, pink face wore a worried, an actively worried, expression, as if knowing that it wasn't the expression required, which should have been responsible, grave, kindly, an expression along those lines. All through the conversation he gave the impression of being simultaneously surprised and at a loss, as if he'd been caught out doing something not exactly against the rules, but against some code he wasn't yet quite grown-up enough to understand. So when he said, once he'd got behind his desk, that he was very sorry, it really did sound as if he was apologising for some misdemeanour of his own, which prevented it from being the chillingly serious opening that he'd probably intended it to be. He probably wanted to start from an absolutely clear understanding of my situation – that it demanded and deserved profound commiserations, and we would proceed from there.

In fact, we didn't seem to be proceeding towards much of consequence. He pretty well repeated what Omar and Morgan Morgan had said – i.e. there were two possibilities: 1) that the tumour on my neck was an independent tumour, the two tumours could be treated separately, in both cases either by surgery or by chemotherapy; 2) that the tumour on the neck was a secondary of the tumour in my lung, which would mean that the cancer cells were in my blood-

71

stream, and the treatment, by radiotherapy, would be palliative, a matter of keeping the cancer in check, but not curing it. The question as to whether we were confronted by 1) or 2) would be answered by the operation to be performed by Dr Morgan Morgan – 'Now, is there anything you want to ask me?' It came out very abruptly, not at all the hesitant invitation of Omar and Morgan Morgan. It was almost a challenge. There was a brief pause, during which he – let me give him a name – Len Rootle let me call him, Dr Rootle – So –

'Now, is there anything you want to ask me?' asked Dr Rootle.

Then came the brief pause. During it he sat behind his desk ogling us. We indicated that there was nothing we wanted to ask him.

'Well,' he said, 'would you like a prognosis? I mean, if the operation to be performed by Dr Morgan Morgan doesn't reveal a cancer in the throat, would you like a prognosis?' It was most peculiar, most peculiar, the way he got this out, awkward, impetuous and alarmed, with a throb of excitement in it.

'No,' Victoria said firmly. No, for her part, she certainly, most certainly didn't want to hear a prognosis.

Dr Rootle nodded inattentively, his ogle was fixed on me.

The word 'prognosis' made me dizzy. Especially as we hadn't yet had a definitive diagnosis, which couldn't be made until after Dr Morgan Morgan's operation, surely – how long would it take them after Dr Morgan Morgan's operation to reach a definitive diagnosis? I wondered.

'How long –' I began, and stopped, thinking that I didn't really want to prolong the conversation, really it was time to go home. Dr Rootle decided that 'How long?' was the whole of my question, which was in response to his own question, so, yes please, he took me to mean, give me your prognosis, how long do I have before I die? 'About a year.' The words came out of the side of his mouth, low but clear.

I believe I said, 'Christ!' I looked at Victoria, who shrank, looked small and white.

I wanted to say, 'But I didn't ask that question, so kindly withdraw your answer.' I also wanted to swear at him, 'You stupid fucking awful fucking moron' sort of stuff, and for a moment or two, as I stared at his face, now for the first time befittingly calm and solemn, with a certain satisfaction in it – 'Mission accomplished! Difficult deed done, and out of the side of my mouth too!' – I wanted to kill him. I wanted to kill him and say just as I pulled the trigger, thrust the dagger, whatever, 'That's a year longer than you have, matey.' The thing I think I understood immediately, before I'd even thought about it, was that a doctor who tells you that you have a year to live has taken the year away from you – from the moment the sentence was delivered – the sentence that delivered the sentence – the knowledge would never be cleared from my consciousness, the last thought at night, the first in the morning, for the rest of my life –

I really don't remember much about how it went after that.

## My Struggle to Escape – Part One

It is one o'clock in the morning, I am sitting at a table on the patio that separates our room from our small private swimming pool, and I am becoming maddened by the walls that hem me in. At the end of the pool there is a row of jagged rocks, cemented together with a gap in the middle to give a view of the sea, which is pitch black. In the morning it's the most marvellous blue, the sea stretches out, you can see boats in the distance, and there is a sense of space, ease, freedom and I leap into the pool, naked, and swim about – this morning, for instance, we went to the beach and swam in the sea, it was almost transparent, it was lovely, then walked back along the garden paths to our room, to find breakfast on the table I am now writing at. I took off my trunks and into the pool I went. It's a saltwater pool, quite cold, cold and cramped, and I don't quite know why I do it, especially after a proper swim in the sea, but it's now become a ritual – sea swim, pool swim, shower, breakfast, and over breakfast the view of the sparkling blue, and the yachts and their sails –

But at night I feel trapped by the walls, the blackness of the sea, so impenetrably black, no lights of passing ships, nothing to distinguish it from the black sky, and my lungs feel as if they are contracting, I begin to cough and wheeze, and panic sets in – panic is setting in now, as I write – I find myself hating the hotel that I like so much in the daytime, and particularly hating the manager –

The wall to the right is so high that it is impossible to see over it. The wall to the left is lower, and if I stand up I can see into the neighbouring pool and the patio and even into a bit of the room next door, and beyond, over their low wall, I can see all the way to the beach, and the little chapel where I sit writing in the daytime, and then the hill above the hotel, with the lights of the cars moving along the roads – the sea is bright, little boats bobbing up and down, and the waves rippling – it is a charming and a painful sight – painful because now I passionately covet the room next to ours that commands this view from its patio, and this morning we were offered it by the manager, and I turned it down. Why did I? Why did he let me? Why didn't he insist on my taking it? What a fool I am! Fool! Sitting here at the table, in my pitch-black cell, my cancer cell – this is hysteria.

That was hysteria.

I calmed down by going to the wall I could see over, the left wall, and breathing in the view, the beach, the little white chapel where I sit, the hills and the lights moving up and down and across. Then I came back here, to the table, and smoked a cigarette.

Now I'm going to write it down in a sensible fashion.

The reason I didn't accept the next-door room that I now covet only just this side of lunacy is because the manager wouldn't let us have a rather splendid bungalow on the other side of the hotel, with accommodation for six people, with the swimming pool set on a large lawn, and most importantly, from the patio where I would sit at night, there was an expansive view of the sea. It's been unoccupied for several days, according to the young

Italian couple in the small suite next to it, and will probably remain unoccupied until the end of the season, and is very expensive, expensive even for four, therefore preposterously expensive for two. I asked the manager if he would give us a discount – no, let's get this absolutely right, for some reason I was worried that he would be upset – his feelings would be hurt – if we wanted to change rooms without explanation, he would think we didn't like our room, which, he'd confided to me, was the best room in the hotel, the one that he, personally, liked the most – he's a rather freaky looking guy, about fifty I suppose, short, with a rosy complexion and glistening black eyes and black plastered-back hair and a high-pitched voice – a lot of Cretans, we've noticed, have high-pitched voices and are quite short – he wears trousers that look as if they're made of tweed, hitched high up on his body, to almost his armpits, and has a rapid, disjointed walk. When we arrived at the hotel last Sunday, at around midnight, it was pouring with rain. A savage wind lashed at us as we got out of the taxi. He came dashing out of the rather grand entrance into the rain and wind to welcome us with an umbrella and to escort us down to an empty restaurant, where a meal had been arranged. The hotel has four restaurants that all close before 11 p.m., which is depressing and completely un-Greek, in our experience, but still, it was thoughtful of him to have a meal ready and waiting, though actually it was spooky, the two of us sitting there in an otherwise totally empty restaurant, the wind howling, the rain beating at the large glass doors.

A very nice man in a suit, plump and avuncular, though about twenty years younger than me, a maître d' figure, I suppose, brought us an assortment of dishes I couldn't eat, so Victoria had to be politely hungry for two. 'Oh, my fran, no food, why no food?' the maître d' kept saying, gazing miserably down at my untouched plate and caressing my shoulder until I was desperate to get away from him, his wounded eyes and the threat of further dishes – perhaps he'd cooked them himself – and said how tired we were, sleepy, and backed it up with imitations of myself sleeping, snoring noises and so forth, but still he insisted on bringing us some terrible Greek puddings. It was a great relief when the manager reappeared, and we could leave the table with fulsome thank yous to the maître d' and scurry after the manager through the rain to our room. It was then that he told me of his love for it, that it was his favourite room etc. and it was just after he'd gone, while Victoria was unpacking, that I took in these oppressive walls. 'We can't stay here,' I said, although it was obvious that we'd have to, at least for the night –

which I got through by taking two sleeping pills, and two co-proxamol, and half a dozen cigarettes. I sat outside on the patio, not completely protected from the rain by a sliver of roofing, and not at all from the wind, which came whistling and howling through or over the walls in a way that seemed quite personal, as if it were seeking me out, in fact. 'Hey! Go get the cancer guy smoking his cigarettes. He's in a daze or a doze from his sleepers. See if you can shake him up a bit. Make him scream out or cry like when we did the old guy back on the heath. See if he's got any "Blow, winds, and crack your cheeks" sort of stuff in him. Cancer, cigarettes, chemicals. Talk about a deserving case!'

At some point before dawn I climbed into bed and clung to my wife.

## My Struggle to Escape – Part Two

It wasn't raining when we woke up, but the wind was still at it, and the skies were grey. In the evening the sun came out, and we had a swim from the little beach. It was surprisingly pleasant in the water, but chilly getting out of it, the wind had dropped a little, but seemed to have become colder, and the few other people on the beach were huddled on sunbeds, under layers of towels. Now and then we discussed the question of changing rooms, then moved on to the question of changing islands, from Crete back to England. If the weather was going to remain like this, what was the point? – confined to a single room, with a cold swimming pool at the end of it? It was a day of depression, really, and of yearning for a few years ago, when I had health, or a few months ago, when I had ignorance.

Then the next day and we were here, saw in its proper weather what a beautiful place it is, so perfectly spread out, with charming walks and so much sea to look at, gentle and kindly, and the surrounding mountains – it was then that I spotted the bungalow, walked up to it, checked it out, and spoke to the Italian couple in the suite next to it – so we went up to the hotel and asked to speak to the manager, hitherto unnamed in these pages, though I remember he'd named himself when he'd first greeted us, in the rain. 'I am Nikos,' he'd said, as he ushered us under his umbrella. 'Is that Mr Nikos?' 'No, no, not Mister, only Nikos, Nikos, so that I can be close to you.' Now he came bustling out of his office in a flurry, clapping his hands and asking how we were, were we happy, could he help? all this in his high, piping voice, his black, marblish eyes slightly at odds with his words – well, as I've said, we couldn't bring ourselves to tell this small man with the pulled-up trousers, plastered-back hair and reedy voice that we didn't like the room he'd put us in, the room he loved most, his favourite in the hotel – instead we went into a fiction we'd concocted that we had friends coming to join us, would need a larger place, really we needed to move to it straight away as these friends never made fixed plans, they turned up when they turned up and we had to be available with accommodation at the ready, what did he have, perhaps one of the rooms on the other side of the hotel, that bungalow perhaps? He said the room next to ours would be free by the end of the day, we would be very near to each other – no, no, we said, we really all had to be in the same quarters, it was our tradition, no, the bungalow would be better, there were certain things we did together at night – actually I was thinking of how when we'd holidayed with James and Dena Hammerstein many years ago, every night we'd played a card game, Hearts, which is a sort of bridge for the retarded, but the way I put it – 'certain things we did together at night' – suggested even less wholesome pursuits, wife-swapping or gay-husbanding and such. He gave me a quick marbly look, perhaps checking on my age, or for evidence of corruption in my face, and said the bungalow would be available in a day or so, and named the preposterous figure. I did something I've never managed to do before. Usually, when told that something I want costs more than I can afford, I smile proudly and take it, a way of affirming my status, I suppose, my financial manhood. But with Nikos I bargained. I said that for much of the time there might only be two of us, indeed our friends were such harum-scarum folk that they were quite likely to arrive after we'd left, so it would be better to proceed on the understanding that there would be just the two. He made a swift calculation.

We could have it with 10 per cent off, the 10 per cent to go straight back on if our friends arrived. He then deducted the 10 per cent out loud, in English, in an impressive display of racing mental arithmetic. When he announced the sum that was left it actually sounded larger than the sum originally proposed – I suppose because the original sum was a round sum, and the amended sum was an awkward sum, which took longer to say. I wondered what his response would have been if I'd said, 'Look, Nikos, according to Dr Rootle I've only eight, nine months at most, to live, couldn't you let me spend two weeks of them in the bungalow at, say, half price?' Instead Victoria and I looked at each other briefly, then said we'd take it, which didn't seem particularly to please him, in fact, he looked slightly fed up, and asked us to phone him with our decision later in the day, and we didn't insist that we'd already made it.

We went down to the beach, had a swim and then considered the matter calmly. Victoria's position was that under the circumstances I was entitled to whatever I wanted, even if we couldn't afford it. As this has been my position for most of my life, it was hard for me to understand why I should resist it now – it may be some sad and childish notion that the more I make myself go without, the more extra time I'll be awarded.

So we rejected the room, and came clean about our reasons for wanting to change. We didn't actually admit that we'd lied about our vagabond friends turning up on the doorstep, but slipped in a query about the availability of a room with a more open view. Victoria spoke movingly about my claustrophobia and my night-time working habits. Visibly controlling his impatience, he led us down all the familiar paths until I felt sure he was going to show us our own room, but he swerved at the last minute and trotted down the steps that led to the next-door room, the one that had the view I had to crane over the wall to enjoy, that got the sun all afternoon – ours went dark well before evening – and had a pool that you could walk around – apart from a brief, narrow strip of paving on the right, ours was hemmed in by the walls – and it was being offered at the same price, he would need to know our decision in half an hour, he had someone waiting for either this room or our room, depending on which one we chose, and with a hitch of his trousers and a cold-eyed smile and a piping farewell he left us to it. Victoria turned the decision over to me, and I – with the proud common sense that has marked such moments in my life – rejected the offer, on the grounds that it was almost certainly the room that would most suit me –

Hence my breakdown, my railings against fate and my intense loathing of the young man – a German, I think, who has moved into it – indeed never moves out of it, his DO NOT DISTURB sign is on permanent display – and he can be glimpsed, through chinks in the wall, lounging naked on the sunbed by the pool – I don't want him to catch me eyeing him through these chinks, reporting me to the management – I'd have to explain to Nikos that it's not lust but homicidal envy that keeps drawing me back to the chinks. On the other hand the way that he lies, so abandoned, with his knees spread apart, suggests that he's an immodest young fellow, or even that he's offering himself to his neighbours, the male or the female, or possibly both. I would say that his face has a depraved and carnal look, but I haven't seen his face yet, am familiar with only the lower part of his body, his private parts, as they used to be called, which he doesn't keep at all private, at least from me, when I happen to glance through the chink.

He's here for the rest of our stay, according to reception, when I phoned to enquire when his room would become available – I've thought of squirting noxious liquids at him through the chink, or perhaps honey, to attract wasps, but I suppose it would be traced to me pretty quickly, and I'd find myself spending my last months in a Cretan prison – or I could try and do it with a kiss, one of the methods prescribed by Oscar Wilde, or like the Chinese woman I read about in the *Herald Tribune* this morning – she murdered her lover by slipping a pellet of rat poison into his mouth while kissing him – it slipped down his throat and into his stomach without his noticing, and he died a few hours later. The woman said at her trial that she and her lover had a pact that if either was unfaithful, the other had the right to kill him or her, and she had noticed him talking in a suspicious manner to a young woman of the village. Apparently murder by rat poison is quite common in China. I suppose it was the decisiveness of her action that impressed and appalled me. I'd bet that the pact was her idea, which he understood to be merely a metaphor for their love, while secretly the thought of it gave him an erotic charge he probably boasted about to his friends – 'She said she'll kill me if I as much as talk to another woman, and I can do the same to her! Hey! What about that!' – but really, from the moment he agreed to the pact his fate was sealed, not only was he bound – honour-bound, in a way – to talk to another woman, she was bound to catch him at it – such a pledge has meaning only if it's fulfilled – and what a kiss it must have been, for him not to notice the pellet in his mouth and then sliding down his throat! – unless of course she'd made a habit of passing something from her mouth to his, to add texture and mystery to a kiss, sometimes a little peppermint or an aphrodisiac, so that he was actually anticipating, his tongue probing eagerly for the expected surprise – but rat poison? I've always imagined death by rat poison to be very painful. Would she have told him, as he writhed in his death throes that she'd merely kept her side of their bargain, so it was his own fault, but oh how she loved him, his present and final agony was a testimony to her love for him. Anyway, she's going to be executed as the Chinese justice system has no place for *crime passionnel*, if that is what it was.

# Opportunity Knocks

This morning after breakfast I was sitting by the pool, thinking about nothing in particular as far as I knew, but Victoria must have seen something in my face because she asked me whether I was all right. I came back from wherever I'd been speaking a jumble of words that made no sense to either of us, and stopped, feeling as bewildered as she looked. These little fits – stupors followed by fluent incoherence – have occurred several times since we've been here, and I don't know whether they're the result of the cancer, the radiotherapy, or simply ageing – a form of Alzheimer's, possibly, though I don't think it's Alzheimer's, or any of its variations. Victoria says that it's probably shock – that I'm still in the process of taking it in. She may be right, but it seems to me odd that I haven't grasped at every level of my being – except in my immortal soul, which will remain delusional until the last possible moment, that's its job after all – that I'm dying. I'm at an age I would have settled for when I was twenty, fifty, even sixty, even sixty-five come to that – and I should have died from alcohol at the end of my drinking life – one more glass would probably have done it. And then there's the smoking. So why should I be surprised, let alone shocked? Yet I think Victoria's right. I was completely unprepared for the news, and still am. Perhaps I am always unprepared, at least when it comes to my health – well yes, consider this, that though you'd been feeling really ill for about a year, you hadn't expected to be told that you were actually ill. Certain events happen annually – Christmas, birthdays, wedding anniversaries – that you have to observe, and in early July, for the last ten years, there have been your medical tests. Yes, it's true that I'd come to treat them as irritating interruptions, and certainly as a formality that had nothing to do with how I actually felt – and why not? as every year the results were pretty much the same, with the sorts of problems that had to do with age – there was cancer of the prostate, but so far it was still in the prostate, and there was an aneurysm that had to be measured and would have to be operated on, but not yet – neither prostate nor aneurysm was treated by the doctors as alarming, and neither was thought about much by me. The tests were a once-a-year humdrummery, and still seemed so this year, although the blood test showed cancerous activity – my GP and my urologist both assumed that it was the prostate cancer stirring at last, but I wasn't to worry, they were prepared, they knew what had to be done and sent me for a scan that would show what the prostate was up to, and also a scan to show how the aneurysm was doing, and also for a scan to make sure that there was no cancer in my bones, and I was having the bone scan, an exceedingly boring business – one has to lie on one's side on a narrow bed while a machine inches over one's body at what seems like ten minutes per inch – I was very tired on the afternoon of the scan, for some reason, but pleased to be so because I fell into a light doze, and stayed there until a disembodied voice roused me with the news that I was done. I got off the bed, put on my clothes, and stumbled out, still a bit sleepy, leaden-limbed and ill at ease. I spotted Victoria standing by a door at the top of the stairs, listening on her mobile. She saw me just as the conversation was evidently finishing. I lumbered towards her, lighting a cigarette as we went out into the alley behind the clinic. 'Who was that?' I said, without much curiosity. She took my hand. I can't remember who it was, or rather which one it was – urologist, GP, aneurysm man, stomach and liver man, all of whom, it turned out, were in possession of the information that one of them had just passed on to Victoria and she was now passing on to me in a voice that was, like her face, calm on the outside. 'They've found something in your lung. On the aneurysm scan.' So not in the prostate, where they were looking for the cause of the cancer activity in the blood tests, but in the lung. It was what they call an 'opportunistic' finding.

So.

So I received the news with mumbled swear words, the words that I was to use quite regularly over the coming weeks and which I've already quoted several times, and are interesting to me, and probably not at all to anyone else, as indications of a poverty of vocabulary in times of crisis, or maybe it's a poverty of actual responses – one simply, no, I simply didn't know what to say when confronted with facts for which I had no reference point – no preparation in myself whatsoever. Even now I wonder if there are moral standards I am failing to meet, and if there are, where am I to find out about them? I can't imagine what I should have said to the first piece of bad news, and the words that spring to mind now are the words that sprang to mind then – but then perhaps such words, along with stupors and bursts of nonsensical eloquence, are the symptoms of shock, and from then on there's been no time, no time –

# A Burst of Adult Behaviour – But Why?

I still can't sort out the following weeks, they were a muddle of scans, consultations, biopsies, further scans, more consultations, until the discovery of a swelling on my neck and the confirmation that it was cancerous – it was odd this, in that it hadn't been there, at least I hadn't noticed it, until the scan detected it, whereupon, as if given permission, it became tangible and visible, a shiny little lump the size of a walnut. Then came the meetings with the three doctors, Omar, Morgan Morgan and Rootle, followed by the hiatus in Suffolk, the long walks in the evening sunshine, the horses in fields that were so green and fresh in an autumn that was like spring, and then the phone call announcing that I had MRSA, then to London for the ghastly operation that established what everybody already knew, that the walnut on the neck was a secondary.

And now here we are in Crete, another hiatus before the next phase begins. When we get back I have to go for a scan to see what effect the radiotherapy has had on the two tumours. All I can say at the moment is that I felt much better before the radiotherapy. In Suffolk I could walk two miles without feeling particularly tired, I could swim eighty-five lengths underwater, I could hurdle fences, I could scuttle up trees and down dales, I could write sonnets in Greek and Latin and translate them into Turkish – I could – but what does it matter what I could do before the radiotherapy? It seems, now, like a dreamtime, as does all my life before Dr Rootle said out of the side of his mouth, 'About a year.'

What occupies me now, as I sit once again with my back against the chapel wall – there is a strong wind, I have to hold the page of my pad down with my left hand as I write, a strong wind and a strong sun, whitecaps racing across the dark blue sea – it's beautiful, really, though the wind is making me shiver a little –

Yes, what occupies me now, as I sit here writing this, is what am I to do with the 'about a year' that is shrinking day by day and now stands at about nine months. What to do with the nine months? In the adult world, represented by novels, films, plays and so forth, people in my position set about 'putting their affairs in order', but I did that very thing, Victoria and I did it, in the months before I learned I was ill. We did it, having postponed it so long – 'We really must,' we kept saying, 'we must really –' until one day, with a sudden sense of urgency, almost somewhat frantically, as if there were a deadline, we began to do it. Neither of us could understand why the urgency, why we chivvied a rather slow, over-careful – so she seemed to us – solicitor with emails and phone calls and faxes, bustled to offices in taxis. When it was complete, as far as we could see, we collapsed with a sort of bewilderment – what, then, was that all about? we asked each other, why all the panic? But still, we said to each other, 'I'm glad we've got it done, aren't you? Now we need never think about it again, now we can relax –'

So now my affairs are in order, there's nothing for me to do unless I change everything on a whim, dis-order them in order to reorder them, like one of those spiteful old people in novels, Miss Havisham for instance – no, I don't think Miss Havisham changed her will, come to think of it, she just implied that it actually contained what Pip's imagination supplied it with. On the other hand, I have so little to leave – the contents of my two studies, one in London and one in Suffolk, and that's about it, apart from my copyrights, not all of which I own, and which are of uncertain value –

## Dialogue Between a Thicko and a Sicko

*How do you value them, as a matter of interest, your copyrights?*

Who?

*You.*

Aka me?

*Yes. Aka you. You personally. You, Simon Gray. The author of your plays. What value do you put on them?*

Financial, do you mean?

*Whatever. Emotional, ethical, sentimental, financial –?*

How can I put a value on my own work? It's for others to do – for others to buy or not buy an option, to stage them or not stage them, and if staged, for other others to say whether they were worth the price of a ticket. The world can tell you the value of my plays by the way it treats them.

*You're lying. You have a very clear idea of whether your plays are any good or not.*

That's not the same thing as how I value them.

*Yes, it is. You're coming to your end, there are going to be obituaries, assessments of your life and work, work and life, by people whose judgements you'd think about if they were being made about somebody else. Now is the chance to put your case.*

My CASE!

*Yup. Go on. Your case. Defend your career as a writer.*

I can't because that's exactly the point I missed, really – that writing is a career. You don't just write and that's the end of it, you have to look after your writing, promote it, cherish it in the world. You have an obligation to get it the help it needs. As people do in all professions – as they do for their children. I was, as far as my work is concerned, a neglectful parent. Furthermore –

*Furthermore?*

Furthermore I suspect that this failure comes from a more profound weakness than mere neglectfulness. Neglectfulness could be, often is, a matter of laziness, or careless impetuosity – 'There, that's finished with, on to the next, and then the next, what's done is done, let it look after itself' sort of attitude – but my neglectfulness was more active than that, it was almost a disowning, and was – is – perhaps still is – the consequence of shame, from

95

which I can never cleanse myself.

*Cleanse yourself?*

Well, you know what I mean.

*No, I don't. Give me some instances.*

Instances! I'm thinking theologically, I can't remember any instances.

*Try, for God's sake!*

Well, let's say my reactions when I happen to over-hear wounding remarks about my work.

*You mean you think you are intended to overhear them? An act of divine will or something, to make you ashamed?*

No, of course not. What I'm talking about is my re-action, not the circumstances. It's merely bad luck or bad judgement that I place myself next to people who then say unpleasant things. I'm not meant to overhear them, after all. I'm sure they'd be horrified if they knew I had. They're as much victims of my bad luck or judgement as I am.

*Are you sure?*

Yes. Of course. You don't think they come looking for me, plant themselves beside me, say these things deliberately for me to hear, do you?

*It's possible.*

It's ridiculous. Give me an instance.

*I thought you didn't want instances.*

Thank you. I knew you couldn't.

*Well, only that taxi driver.*

What taxi driver?

*The one who came to pick you up when you were a lecturer at Queen Mary College, in the East End, to take you home to Highgate.*

Lots of taxi drivers came to pick me up at Queen Mary and take me home to Highgate.

*You saw this one talking to the porter when you went to find him at reception. Surely you remember.*

I left both Queen Mary and Highgate twenty years ago, how could I possibly remember!

*They both looked at you as you were coming towards the desk. The taxi driver said something and the porter laughed.*

He had a wart on the back of his neck, did he?

*Which one?*

The driver, of course.

*So you do remember?*

I am now in the process of remembering it. The moment you mentioned the wart, you set my memory off. Memory is a creative faculty. I am a creative writer. It only takes one small thing, one detail. Your wart was my madeleine, so to speak.

*It's not my wart, it's yours. I didn't remember it, I didn't mention it. You did.*

Oh. Well – well – it's not surprising, is it, as it's all I had of him in the back of his cab, the wart on his neck, and his voice.

*Saying –*

What?

*What was he saying?*

Oh, only that – that he'd been to see my play –

*He and his wife. Don't leave out his wife. So – he and his wife – they'd been to see your play* Otherwise Engaged *the night before and – and –*

He was rather abusive.

*But what exactly, mmm?*

Oh, just the usual sort of thing. That he hadn't cared for it. So forth.

*Really? They hadn't cared for it? Those were his words?*

That was his meaning.

*He gave you an honest opinion. He spoke his mind. Is that what you mean by abusive?*

I didn't ask him to give his opinion. Or to speak his mind.

*Still, it's pretty mild, 'didn't care for it'. Now if he'd said something like, 'It was terrible, terrible, terrible, my missus said we should ask for our money back, what a waste of money, she said, what a waste of an evening, the only evening we've had out for months, a disgrace, how does a thing like that get on the stage, and at those prices!' – if he'd said something like that – did he?*

Possibly along those lines.

*And how did you silence him?*

I didn't dignify him with a response. I was almost certainly trying to concentrate on an upcoming lecture – probably on Wordsworth, I lectured on Wordsworth most terms, I could do a whole hour on the 'Lucy' poems, half an hour alone on 'A slumber did my spirit seal;/I had no human fears:/She seem'd a thing that could not feel/The touch of earthly years./No motion has she now, no force;/She neither hears nor sees;/Roll'd round in earth's diurnal course' –

99

*'As for the bastard who wrote that shit! What wouldn't I give to get my hands on him!' – Sorry, didn't mean to interrupt, probably a rotten imitation, eh? I don't think I caught the note of delirious venom, astonished joy – that he actually had the bastard who wrote the shit in the back of his cab – the sheer luck of it!*

And what about the sheer luck of it for me? I phone for a taxi and of all the drivers available in London I get the only one, surely the only one, who'd gone to my play the night before – he has a chance conversation with the porter – says to the porter, for want of anything else to say, that he'd had a – a – rather disappointing night at the theatre – and the porter says –

*'Here comes the man you're looking for, the very man that wrote the shit!' You think that sort of coincidence is luck, do you, simple bad luck? It's not just a case of standing next to somebody in a pub, or hearing somebody as they're leaving the theatre. As you've said yourself, so many different elements came together.*

What do you think it is?

*You tell me. You're the theologian. The shame-seeker. The man who needs a good cleansing. Perhaps it was you who sought him out, not the other way around.*

How could I? How could I possibly? The odds were

hundreds of thousands to one – possibly millions – unless you think I phoned for a taxi and said, by the way, I want a driver who took his wife to *Otherwise Engaged* last night and hated it.

*Not heavy odds against the last bit. Perhaps he was the answer to your prayers, as you were to his. He wanted the bastard who wrote the shit in the back of his cab, you wanted the humiliation, the shame – God works in mysterious ways to get these match-ups. You've fallen strangely silent, as Mummy used to say to Daddy when she'd embarrassed him. Well, it's only me, not even Mummy. You can't be embarrassed by only me.*

I'm not embarrassed. I'm trying to work it out. The truth is that I didn't feel abused, I felt unmasked. Yes, that's the truth.

*That he was right? Your play was shit? You deserved, as well as needed, to hear it? Eh?*

Yes, but – whether *Otherwise Engaged* was shit or not is irrelevant. In my soul –

*Your soul?*

Soul, yes – don't worry about the word, it's theological jargon, as is the rest of what I'm about to say. In my soul I believe I am one of the fallen, and that my natural and proper condition in the world is that of a man who needs –

*Cleansing?*

Yes.

*Well, go on, on into shame, humiliation, the rest of it. Your voice is developing that throb. It's your confessional voice. You've got a palpable design on my emotions, haven't you, you little devil you!*

I hate anyone – anyone! – who has a palpable design on the emotions, you know I do.

*Even a child?*

Children don't.

*Really? Too innocent?*

Yes – well, let's say too ignorant.

*I know a child. Let me tell you about him. The sort of thing he used to do. An* instance, *if you like, of the sort of thing he used to do.*

It's a beautiful day. I'd really rather –

*It'll only take a minute. Have a cigarette. Go on. You need and deserve one, just the one. One can't hurt you. Here. Let me light it for us.*

# A Child with a Palpable Design

*It is 1942. He is standing on a street corner in downtown Montreal, outside a post office. He has a letter in his hand, to send to his parents back there in England, and he is upset because he can't find the money his Auntie Gert had given him for the stamp. He begins to cry. A grown-up stops to ask the little chap what the matter is, and he explains, holding up the envelope. The grown-up smiles at how small mishaps seem great tragedies for children, rumples the little chap's hair, gives him money for the stamp, and a little bit over, from the pleasure of giving. After the little chap had posted the letter he went home, thought awhile then, without consulting his older brother Nigel, wrote another envelope, returned to the corner and burst into tears. Men and women stopped regularly to ask him what the matter was. He showed them the envelope, told them he'd lost the money for the stamp for the letter for his mummy and daddy in England. It was amazing what delicate chords he touched in passers-by. In time he grew bold and impatient. Instead of standing passively shedding tears and waiting to be consoled and rewarded, he began to accost people, holding out the envelope, sobbing and asking if they could help him, his letter to his mummy and his daddy, in England – well, a weeping* child, his parents in the war-torn and valiant mother country, he stoppeth one in nine, or eight, even, and even a very large, ill-tempered-looking man striding along, who nevertheless paused to enquire tenderly, 'What's the matter, son?' and the little chap trembled and whimpered out his answer, whereupon the large man, looking no longer ill-tempered, lowered himself to the little chap's height and cupped his vast hands around the little chap's cheeks, smiled into the little chap's eyes and informed the little chap that he was a policeman, and if it wasn't that he was off duty and going home, he'd take the little chap down to the station and have him put in jail for swindling, fraud, etc. He stood up and addressed the passers-by, 'Don't give money to this kid, he's a liar! A liar and a cheat! I'd arrest him if I had the time!' and went on his way back to his family, a Samaritan of some sort, and the little chap ran home, doubtless thinking that, well, all good things come to an end, his pockets were full of money for cigarettes, candy, comics – so how's that for a child with a palpable design? And not only on the emotions but on the emotions for the money? Pretty well what he did when he grew up and became a playwright, eh? Same sort of trick, when you think about it – and same sort of comeuppance, except it comes from critics, and not from a policeman.

You've missed out the real end of the story. I ran home in a shock of shame. A shock. Of shame.

*Because you were caught.*

Of course. But also for what I'd done. The two things were mixed into each other. I knew that I deserved –

*And needed – don't forget needed – you deserved and needed to be caught, right? Just as you deserved and needed to get bad reviews, right? And deserved and needed to be abused by the cab driver, right? And so deserved and needed to get cancer is the next thought, eh? Right?*

## The Next Thought

Well, actually, it's not quite as if cancer were an off-duty policeman and I a swindling child, but not altogether not that – there is certainly a sense of shame that makes me feel that I'm at a moral disadvantage when discussing my condition – I have been caught out, they (the doctors) have caught me out – but in what? Well, of course in my smoking, but really, when it comes to it, I don't believe my cancer is the result of smoking, or rather the much more important question is what my smoking is the result of. What in my nature made me a smoker? What in my nature allows me – sometimes it feels more like insistence – to go on smoking? The thought of dying terrifies me, the thought of dying of cancer particularly terrifies me, and yet – and yet – destiny is too grand a word, what I want is a word that has the meaning of a meeting up between the something in me that needs to smoke, call it a genetic disorder or call it original sin, and the something in me that needs the consequence, call it an effect, as in the law of cause and effect, or a punishment. When it comes to thoughts of this sort, this contradictory sort, I remember that not only am I a great-great-grandchild of the Enlightenment, which was itself the father of chaos, but also that I'm descended on my father's side from a long line of Scots Presbyterians, on my mother's from a long line of Welsh Anglicans, i.e. Anglicans who, because of their Welshness, believed in sin, original sin and sin ever since. In other words, what a mess.

One of my fears in life has always been that other people are as bad as I am. Then what hope for the world? I think. What's more –

*Hey – no more 'what's more's' and 'furthermore's', all this stuff about guilt, shame, sin, in fact all the stuff since I asked you your opinion of your contemporaries, it's all evasion.*

Actually, you asked me for my opinion of myself. And I gave it.

*No, you didn't. You went into an account of how you'd*

*mishandled your career. You claimed it was from a holy innocence, an innate and genuine belief in the need to behave with integrity –*

No, I didn't. I said it was from stupidity, a failure to understand what the world is, how it works. There are two entirely unrelated activities. One is writing, the other is getting on in the world. There is nothing shameful in knowing how to get on in the world and there is something shameful in my not knowing – it's wilful. And vain in the sense of conceited ignorance, the assumption that my modesty will come to be associated with my work, almost a subtle manifestation of its virtues.

*But if you're going to be dead soon, then the sooner you stop suppurating about the injustices and dishonesties of the world – of which you claim you're a victim – the more time you'll have to suppurate about the things that matter. Like the triumphs of your contemporaries.*

I'm not suppurating about anything. That's what I'm trying to tell you. If you listen to me properly you'll hear the voice of a man who is learning to accept his death with composure and even serenity.

*Then why does it squeak?*

It's a physical thing, in my lungs. Not a psychological thing. I want to talk about Chekhov.

*Chekhov?*

Yes, Chekhov.

*Would you like to run with that?*

Well, his plays are about – oh, you know – love and the failure of love, friendship and the failure of friendship, about brotherhood and parenthood, about the work people do, how they see themselves, their fear of how others see them, their fear of loss, illness and death. That sort of play.

*And politics?*

Politics?

*Chekhov had an interest –*

Some of his characters did. They had visions of the future, yearnings for the past. But there was censorship, of course, that defined the limits of discussion. But no one, I hope, comes out of a Chekhov play talking first of all about the light it sheds on Russia at the turn of the century, although you might get around to that in due course – see it in relation to the Revolution etc., but in the end it's the feeling that every conversation in the plays is somehow *sub specie aeternitatis* that makes them now funny and now sad, often both at once.

*So you think of yourself as Chekhovian?*

Not in the usual meaning of the word, which is to do with atmosphere, the mixture of the touching, the comic and the melancholy, *fin de siècle*, I suppose one could call it, that meaning of Chekhovian – but I aspired to write plays, dreamed of writing plays that leave audiences with the experience of having looked in on other lives, other conditions, and have them see much that's the same as and much that's different from their own lives. All I'm really saying is that sort of theatre seems to me true theatre, in that sense Chekhovian, the kind of plays that I tried to write, and wish I'd written.

*Well now, perhaps you'll come out with it.*

With what?

*How you value yourself.*

I think I'm better than my reputation. Possibly I'm the best playwright in English of the second half of the last century, well, at writing the sorts of plays I wanted to write, but then I suspect that nobody else wanted to write those sorts of plays, so being the best at it –

*What about some titles?*

*Quartermaine's Terms, Close of Play, The Common*

109

*Pursuit, The Rear Column, The Late Middle Classes, Japes* and so forth.

*And so forth? What about the two early plays, the ones that made you briefly rich, and more briefly famous?* Butley *and* Otherwise Engaged.

Yes, well I'm not denying them. They were revived recently, *Otherwise Engaged* in the West End and *Butley* on Broadway. Both were well received and played to good houses and it was quite pleasant to be in the audience, but I didn't really feel they had much to do with me, I've lost contact with the man who wrote them, I've no idea, really, what they came out of, they seem to be about waste, self-waste and partly self-disgust. But I may be quite wrong, they may be about something else entirely. All I really remember is being astonished by their success at the time. And also by the anger they aroused. One theatre critic, I think of the Oxford newspaper – both plays had their premieres in Oxford – wrote that he hoped to meet up with me so that he could punch me in the stomach. And I got some letters from women along the same lines, though knees into balls was more how they looked forward to greeting me. It must have been the climate of the times, there was nothing of that sort of response in the recent revivals, or if there was, it wasn't passed on to me.

*But the later plays* – Quartermaine's Terms, Close of Play, The Common Pursuit, The Rear Column, The Late Middle Classes, Japes *and so forth – you're still in touch with the man who wrote those?*

Yes. But less so and less so. I'm losing touch with – Excuse me.

*Where are you going?*

For a swim.

*But we haven't finished.*

I have. It's a lovely afternoon, and I can't afford to spend it on a grubbing journey through my work, defending and puffing it, what will survive will survive and so forth, and whether it does or doesn't I shall never know and there's the sea, all a-sparkle, and there'll be Victoria down there on her sunbed, half waiting for me, and I may not have many more afternoons like this, not many more swims with my wife, *carpe diem, carpe diem*!

## Back Trouble

It's been three days since I've written, three days of sunshine and cool, calm evenings. I've become languorous and physically at ease, I have no sense that there is anything wrong with my body at all, apart from my slight hack of a cough, which is infrequent and socially much less noticeable than the coarse and liquid brute that used to revolt those around me. I've been swimming about six times a day, and furthermore I haven't smoked until the evening, when I smoke ten, well, say a dozen to be on the safe side, as opposed to the old sixty or more a day, could this be one of the reasons I've been feeling better? so much better that I don't want to ruin it by writing about the second meeting with Dr Rootle, without which this record of my recent medical history is incomplete. Every time I've thought of beginning, pulling my yellow pad towards me and picking up my pen, I settle back for a moment against the chapel wall, and drift, drift along, leaving Dr Rootle and his importunate knees – he sat so close to me while he talked that our knees almost touched – well, as I put that down I feel myself inclined to sit back again, put down the pen, push the pad away and drift, drift, and think anyway that it's nearly lunchtime, time for another swim, we like to have three before lunch, but as yet haven't been in since our pre-breakfast dip, hours ago, hours and hours ago it now seems, though in fact it's only – what? two

112

and a half hours. Perhaps in a minute I shall write about Dr Rootle.

We had dinner again at the restaurant by the chapel. Only three of the other tables were taken, and the people at them were as low-voiced as we were. It was a lovely still evening, a perfect temperature for eating out, the moon bright and the sea shimmering. We talked of this and that, comfortably but not altogether aimlessly. Underlying all our conversations is the thought of the future, but on the whole we try to stay away from it, so I don't really know why I suddenly began to talk about the way I wanted certain things disposed of, those copyrights I still own and one or two items, not valuable but with a meaning for me, and I hope for the people I want them to go to – then my back began to hurt, as it has done occasionally since the radiotherapy. I got up, walked about, then went to the railing and looked out over the sea, listening to the waves – it was the most soft and gorgeous evening, I forgot what I'd been saying, and turned to go back to the table, to say to Victoria come, come and have a look at this! when I saw that her head was bent and she had a hand to her face – I suppose it was the matter-of-factness of my manner, the assumption, and the assumption that she shared it, that my death is fairly soon and inevitable – but the truth is that I don't really know even quite elementary things about myself, my wants and needs, until I've either written them down or spoken them – still, it was very thoughtless of me, stupid, stupid – I couldn't get through this, if that's what I'm doing, without her, I couldn't have done anything over the last twenty years without her, I've for so long taken what sureness and confidence I have from her undemonstrative strength that I don't ever think what a strain it must be for her, and now more than ever – I must be more careful, must be more careful – but she wouldn't want me to be careful, would she? so I must also be careful not to seem careful.

## Reflections of a Smoking Anti-smoker

I suppose I should remind myself that I smoked one or two cigarettes at the restaurant last night, something I swore to myself I wouldn't do while we're in Crete, and that I will no longer be able to do in restaurants in England – well, not strictly accurate, it'll be permitted at tables outside – here you can smoke inside too – I can see from here that in the restaurant, in the enclosed bit, there are ashtrays on the tables, two on each table.

It's astonishing how quickly strange new social

customs are developing in London because of the ban – for instance, at Kensington Place the table we always sit at is next to the window and beside the revolving door, so I have a comfortable view of diners who now go out to smoke on the pavement – some of them go to the bus stop a few yards down the road, because it has a bench to sit on and a bit of roof to protect them when it's raining – others go round the other side to an alley, and are usually out of sight – but quite a few can't be bothered to go anywhere, they stay right by the restaurant window in clusters, sometimes so close to our table that only the pane of glass separates us. I'd never realised before how unattractive groups of people are who are only there for the smoke. I suppose it's because they're not doing something else while smoking, or smoking without noticing, as they used to, they're there for one purpose only, to smoke, and it makes smoking a bit disgusting – after all, it's an activity that should be subsidiary to other activities, and to do it for its own sake makes it seem like an affliction or a degrading personal habit. Like nose-picking for instance, it should be done in the utmost privacy, and though it's possible that all kinds of exciting things – engagements, adulteries, divorces and even murder – might follow on from accidental relationships formed on the pavement, it most often looks a dismal and solitary affair, people who don't know each other standing apart, heads bent over their cigarettes with a shifty or an agitated air, as if they were outside a courtroom, awaiting the verdict and sentencing. Mainly that's the social effect one notices of the smoking ban, the outside-on-the-pavement effect, but the other day, at a fairly large dinner party – about twenty people or so, also at Kensington Place – I noticed for the first time the inside-the-restaurant effect – it was really a very pleasant evening, everything seeming to be going well and comfortably, the people knew each other, the food was good, the wine was flowing, the chattering and laughter festively loud, when suddenly one of the men stood up, looked around the table in a knowing manner, and raised two fingers to his mouth in a smoking gesture, whereupon about eight people – five or six men and a couple of women – got up and trampled out in a little pack or herd, pack is probably the right word, inasmuch as a self-appointed leader had given the signal. Several people were left stranded at the table with empty chairs on either side of them, one woman had no one on either side of her and no one opposite her either, it was as if she were being ostracised, or in quarantine – she sat there smiling in a falsely dignified sort of way, what else could she do? After about ten minutes the pack, no, herd seems the right word here, because in they trampled like cattle, though they didn't look sheepish, which would have been appropriate, but as if they thought they were charmingly naughty, which also made them seem rather pleased with themselves. Eventually the table picked up, everything flowed along until there he was on his feet again and with his fingers to his lips. It happened twice more during the evening, and I felt – I have to admit it – that their behaviour was – well, loutish. And selfish, actually. Of course it's easy for me, in that my lung cancer makes me positively relieved to be in places where I'm not allowed to smoke, but I hope, I really do hope, that even if I were healthy and back on sixty a day I would have remained seated until the end, looking forward to smoking when I got home – but alas, alas, alas and further alas, I have a ghastly feeling that not only would I have gone out to the pavement, but I would have competed for leadership of the pack – or herd, whichever – and no doubt thought myself naughty and charming, while in fact being selfish and loutish.*

Oddly, or perhaps not oddly, come to think of it, the

* A short while after writing this I joined the smokers on the pavement. However, I have not yet thought myself naughty and charming.

117

smoking ban came into effect about three days after I discovered I'd got cancer. Yes, now I do come to think of it, it seems more than odd, it seems eerily consequential, suggesting among other possibilities that I am so innately, organically obedient that my whole physical system submitted to the law in spite of my habits and inclination, and that my inner opposition to it was immediately met by the most appropriate and natural punishment.

On the night before you could no longer smoke inside a restaurant we had a long-prearranged dinner with Ronald and Natasha Harwood, smokers of a quantity and intensity to equal my own, at a restaurant in Piccadilly, one of the very few restaurants that still allowed smoking right up to the last day – a lot of restaurants had introduced their own ban months before – so it was on that night a particularly popular spot, they'd put three or four ashtrays on each table, and the clientele all had their cigarettes and lighters on display in a here-we-stand spirit, perhaps there was even a flavour of Dunkirk about it, heroic and defiant defeat. Now, the thing was that at that time I really couldn't bear to smoke, each inhalation made me dizzy and nauseated, but the desire – the need – to smoke was as strong as ever, and the knowledge that I had lung cancer made me – what was it? Defiant? No, no. I think anxious to show that nothing of major importance had changed in my life, so not defiant, stupid. Stupid to sit there with lung cancer smoking cigarettes I didn't want and that made me feel sick for a cause I no longer believed in – the cause being the right of smokers to fill a restaurant with smoke and a smell that many people can't abide, and makes some of them feel actually ill.

So it was altogether a weird evening at the place in Piccadilly, it was the Wolseley I now remember, of course it was the Wolseley, spent with very good friends whose company I always enjoy – a weird and also horrible evening, the evening before the first day of the smoking ban, the last evening when it was still legal to smoke inside restaurants and people hadn't yet developed the habit of standing on the pavement and irritating diners by the windows as they do at Kensington Place.

Actually, there are very few restaurants that have windows as large as Kensington Place, where all the diners, not only the ones sitting next to the window, can see out on to Kensington Church Street, and everyone in Kensington Church Street – pedestrians, as well as people in cars, buses and taxis – can see into the restaurant, can actually see quite distinctly the faces of the diners with our snouts in our troughs and the waiters scurrying about, obedient to our appetites. It's a sight that could start a revolution. Who, if poor, hungry, unemployed, wouldn't feel like heaving a brick through the window? lots of bricks through the window? the thought of all that glass shattering, splinters flying into our bowls of soup, our venison, our puddings, our faces – and then the mob unleashed, hurdling through the holes with more bricks for close-up and personal. In fact, the more I think about it the more I wonder whether it's safe and sensible to sit at our particular table. It's quite difficult not to catch the eye of pedestrians, and indeed sometimes a pair or a trio of yobs pause, rap their fists on the windows and dance jigs and pantomime obscenities. We try to smile aloofly back at them, as if we were at a distance and invulnerable – I think we ought to find out whether the glass is shatterproof, whether bricks would bounce off it or smash through it. If the latter what should we do? Take our custom to a restaurant with smaller windows? Or, less radically, move to one of the tables on the other side, against the wall, which no brick, however powerfully thrown, could reach? And yet – and yet the charm of our table is its location, we're slightly cut off from the other tables and have the best acoustics, we enjoy watching the parade through the vast windows in spite of being threatened and jeered at by intoxicated louts and – and you must stop this, what have smokers outside Kensington Place and imaginary yobs throwing bricks through the window got to do with what's happening to you and where you are? Why not think about our being here, the simple pleasure of our being here in Crete?

Right. Tomorrow back in Crete.

No, tomorrow back to Dr Rootle. Your last meeting.

Then you can have Crete.

## Dr Rootle's Knees

His secretary summoned us to a meeting at the hospital, to a different waiting room, very large, with several coffee machines and a counter where you could buy sandwiches and chocolate bars. It had several doors, from which elegant, usually Asian nurses would appear, call out a name, and somebody would rise eagerly and hurry forward. It wouldn't have seemed at all like a hospital waiting room if there weren't so many people, of all ages, with sticks and crutches, bandages on their wrists and ankles, the most striking being those who had bandages around their necks with a circular hole in front, and a bit of tube that obviously went into the throat. There was a bulky and frankly rather brutish-faced man and, like a biker in a film, he had cropped hair, tattoos on his arms, a black leather waistcoat and black leather trousers. Although he was very big, massive biceps and a bull neck, he was quite unmenacing. I don't think it was just the circumstances that made him unmenacing. He had a soft, slightly abstracted smile and a vague, unseeing but rather tender way of looking around at the rest of us as he waited on his partner, a raddled-looking woman in a shapeless yellow dress, with stringy black hair and a peaky face, and most noticeably a throat bandage with a plug in it – he kept bringing her various items from the counter, a mug of coffee and then a sandwich, which she put in her pocket, and then a chocolate bar, and then another chocolate bar, one of which she put in her pocket, the other she shared with him. They also each had a packet of cigarettes, Marlboro, and a lighter each, which they kept on the arms of their chairs, very visibly, but seemingly quite unconscious of the – what? inappropriateness, I suppose is the right word – in the waiting room of a famous cancer hospital, with those signs all around showing struck-off cigarettes, and strategically placed racks with pamphlets announcing the relationship between smoking and cancer – and yet there they were, sitting beside their cigarettes. At one point he said something to her and they both opened their packets and began to count the contents with their fingers, he plucked two of his out and gave them to her, she squeezed one of them into her packet, which seemed already pretty full from where I sat, and kept the other one between her fingers – there was an exciting little passage when he picked up the lighter as if to light her cigarette, but he just bounced it up and down on his palm, whispering endearments to her, and she nodded and nodded, it was hard to keep one's eyes off the cigarette between her fingers, the black tube in her throat – I wondered if she could speak, and also wondered whether she actually smoked, and if she did, did she plug the cigarette into the plug in her throat? It didn't bear thinking about, really. And nor did the fact that I had a packet of Silk Cut and a lighter in my own pocket, and as soon as we were out of the hospital I would light up – would I, if I ever had to have a plug in my throat, would I even then? When I was called at last, by an exceptionally neat and pretty Chinese nurse, the man smiled in his pleasant, slightly absent way, and put his hand on the woman's, as if to say, 'Your turn soon,' and she –

No, time for a swim.

It's past midnight, and I'm on the patio, one hand

clamped on my pad to keep the pages down in the strong wind, which I'm determined to ignore because I want to pick up where I left off, before our swim. Actually, it wasn't much of a swim, this wind had already –

No. To the meeting.

The nurse led us down a corridor and showed us into a small room, in which there were three chairs – no, two chairs, one with a stool in front of it. The nurse said, 'Dr Rootle will be with you shortly,' and went, leaving the door into the corridor open. There was another door, which wasn't quite closed, into another room, from which came men's voices, loud, jolly, slightly argumentative. Their voices also came at us along the corridor, so that they were twice as loud as they would have been with only one of the doors open, but they somehow overlapped and drowned themselves out. It was almost as if they were in the room with us, shouting out incomprehensible sentences, it was impossible to make out any word clearly except one, which seemed to detach itself and ring out separately. My name. Every few seconds, in the excited, humorous babble, a cocktail party sort of babble, my name, followed once or twice by a little silence, and then a murmur, a little laugh. This went on for about ten minutes, it was quite hellish, until at last Victoria cried out, 'We can hear you!' in fact cried it out several times, but there wasn't a flutter of silence or uncertainty from the next room, the shouting, the laughter, the good-humoured quarrelling continued at full throttle, even when she went out into the corridor and called out from there. We'd pretty well decided that we'd show ourselves at one of the doors – simultaneously, one at each door, might have been a better idea – when the voices stopped and almost immediately Dr Rootle strode exuberantly into the room by the connecting door, followed seconds later by Dr Morgan Morgan from the corridor door – virtually doing to us what I've just imagined doing to them. There was some fervent hand-shaking in a muddled sort of way – it really was a small room, too small for four people to do the social things without jostling each other – and then Dr Morgan Morgan said he was just looking in for a moment to say hello, then he'd leave us, leave us – he gestured to Dr Rootle – but first if he could just glance – just a quick glance – into my throat, to make sure that the operation – I sat there with my wife to one side of me, Dr Rootle to the other, while Dr Morgan Morgan went down my throat for a quick glance, and then came up again, and said, he really did say, I had some difficulty believing it, and still do, he said, 'The good news is that it's all clear down there, not a sign of anything wrong, and there was no cancer in the tonsil I took out, it was just slightly infected.' And I said again, I really did say, though I had no difficulty believing it, 'But that's not exactly good news, is it? It would have been better if it had been cancerous, the tonsil, wouldn't it?' 'Ah,' he said, 'well, there is that.' He offered me his hand, and I shook it. He offered it to Victoria, who shook it. 'Now,' he said, smiling shyly at Dr Rootle, 'over to you, um,' and off he went, out into the corridor and then on to the canteen or to a ward or to a woman or to his wife, closing the door behind him. Dr Rootle closed the door into the other room, then sat down on the stool in front of me. As I've mentioned elsewhere, I think, our knees almost touched. Also he leaned forward, so that his face was close to mine. I could feel his breath on my face, wholesome and clean – I was anxious about my own, that it wasn't full of nicotine and other impurities. As he was on the stool, he was lower than me, but I had the impression that he was towering above me. I felt myself hunching, like a schoolboy having an unhappy session with his hyperactive housemaster – I've discovered that being told you're dying sometimes distorts your view of people, you sometimes feel very small, which makes them seem very large. I was completely hypnotised and cowed by Dr Rootle's physical proximity, he was all teeth and

spectacles, large, gleaming teeth and flashing spectacles, and there were his knees, I had to force myself
not to look down at them as he spoke in a warm,
clear and urgent fashion – all I really took in was that
he'd arranged for me to start a course of radiotherapy quite soon. He explained what its purpose was,
what effect it would have, and other stuff which I
hoped Victoria was assimilating. The one thing I
managed to grasp was that he didn't once mention
his previous prognosis, that he was confining himself to my immediate future, and that he managed
to make it sound pretty lively, and when Victoria
asked him whether it would be all right to go away
on a holiday, he said enthusiastically that yes, why
not if I felt well enough, just go on doing all the
things I usually do, why not? – that came right at the
end, before he got up and left the room.

'Is it over?' I asked Victoria, who smiled comfort-
ingly as if she'd understood everything, which she
evidently had, because she said, 'No, no, he's just
gone to sort out the dates for the radiotherapy.'

'Did he ask us if we wanted to ask him anything?'

'No.'

When he came back he had a paper in his hand,
with the dates, days, hours and venue on it, and
handed it to Victoria – clearly he'd understood the
difference between the person he was obliged to

talk to and the one who understood what he was saying. When they'd finished there was one of those short, uncertain pauses that precede good-byes between people who don't know each other, then he said to Victoria, 'If there's anything you think I can help you with, don't hesitate to get in touch,' and gave her his email address. They shook hands. He turned to me, held out his hand, and as I took it, in all its capability and power, the hand of a grown man, a true adult, he rested his other hand on my shoulder and said, gently, almost sotto voce, 'Don't worry. We'll take care of you.'

Afterwards, sitting at a lopsided table on the awkward chairs outside the pub, Victoria took me through my appointments, which were to begin the following Tuesday, when I would have my chest and neck marked with little tattoos, to show where the rays had to be aimed, then Wednesday, Thursday and Friday and the following Monday and Tuesday for the actual radiotherapy. I remember we felt relaxed, almost jolly. Victoria's eyes were bright and so was her voice, possibly my own were too – and this wasn't simply because I hadn't taken in most of what he'd said, because Victoria had explained it to me on the way out of the hospital, it was all quite simple and unthreatening, the treatment might hurt slightly, causing a burning sensation at the spots where the rays penetrated, but then again it might not. I would be likely to feel tired for a week or two after the treatment, but would then begin to feel better, much, much better.

'But better than what? I haven't been feeling ill.'

'Even so, you could probably feel better.'

This was undeniably true. One could always feel better, and there was a strong possibility that I'd got so used to feeling ill that I no longer noticed it.

We stayed at the pub for quite a while, free of tension, in fact quite uplifted – a tribute on Victoria's part to Dr Rootle's energy and confidence, and on mine to his physical and moral dominance. I felt such relief at having escaped from it, yes, exactly like a schoolboy who'd learned that there was to be no punishment after the interview, that the interview itself was the punishment – if indeed it was a punishment, it might even have been intended as a benefit. We went on to discuss our holiday. We'd have almost four clear weeks before we had to be back, there was a christening that we absolutely had to go to, Toby and Annie-Lou Stephens's newborn son, Eli. We'd been asked to be his godparents, were honoured to be asked. After that there would be the scan that would show what effect the radiotherapy had had.

I smoked a cigarette or possibly even two during this, as we decided that we'd go to Greece, but where in Greece? Perhaps to our usual island, Spetses – but Spetses wasn't reliable in its weather in early October, it could be beautiful, warm but fresh, the sea at its most perfect for swimming – I wasn't sure I was up to Spetses emotionally, if it turned out to be as lovely as we hoped, with the soft light fading in the evening, and all the familiar people in the familiar bars and cafés, it might feel like a leave-taking, harrowing – so what about Crete? – yes, Crete, we'd look into Crete, we'd been there once in early summer and liked it, and it was known to be at its best late in autumn and we had no ties to it, we could just enjoy it for what it was. I had a severe thought, and presented it to Victoria. 'Look,' I said, 'do you think it's quite right for me to be Eli's godfather, given my situation? Shouldn't he have somebody who's likely to be around for him? I mean, that's the point of a godfather.' She was unusually sharp with me, saying that Toby and Annie-Lou had been aware of my 'situation' when they asked me, they wanted me to be a godfather, that's all there was to it. She didn't say, 'Subject closed,' but it was. Anyway, I remembered that Toby and Annie-Lou were Catholics, there were probably all kinds of contingency plans in their church, an edict or a bull could sort the matter out, when the time came.

Just before we left, or it might have been when we were on our way to the car, I said, 'What did he mean, they'll take care of me? "Don't worry, we'll take care of you," he said. And he put his hand on my shoulder. What did he mean by it?' Victoria said she hadn't heard him say it. 'He said it in a low voice. When he put his hand on my shoulder.' She said that he certainly didn't mean anything sinister by it, he certainly only meant that he'd make sure I got the right treatment. Still, the phrase and the gesture troubled me, as they do now that I think about them, sitting here, on the patio, at two in the morning. The wind's dropped, it's quite still, and through the break in the wall I can see a small boat in the moonlight, just the one, rocking gently, and a dark figure bunched at the end, by the bow, fishing I suppose – I can't see clearly what he's doing, he may be asleep, or just sitting, possibly watching me. I must be very visible, because I got the management to clamp a couple of extra lamps to the roof, angled to shine down on the patch where this table is – yes, he can certainly see me if he's looking in this direction, see what I look like and what I'm doing. I think I'll stop writing now, have a cigarette and just sit, watching the boat, and hope that he stands up and moves about, that he waves to me. I'd like that.

# The Bundles on the Beach

The beach looked completely deserted at 9 a.m. this morning when we had our swim, except for two bundles of clothing on adjacent sunbeds that had been left behind from the evening before, or had been put down as markers, to reserve the places until the day got warmer. There was an autumnal nip in the air, which is perhaps why there was no one else on the beach, or it might be that a lot of guests left yesterday evening and will be replaced by a new lot tonight, when the planes come in from London, Manchester, Paris, Milan –

We had our swim, quite a brief one, and headed for the shower, passing on our way the two beds with the bundles of clothing on them, which turned out to be two elderly women – quite a bit older than me, into their eighties, I should think – in their overcoats, collars up to their chins, scarves wrapped around their necks and more scarves over their feet. They both wore glasses and were both smoking. One of them was curled on her side, and nestled against her stomach was a dachshund. 'Good morning!' we said to them, wet, cold, but unfailingly polite, as many English feel obliged to be, when abroad, to show that we don't intend to punch and kick people just because they're old and on a beach, for instance. I added a loving chuckle for the dog. The two ladies looked at us not exactly with malevolence, but with hostility and a soupçon of contempt, then spoke to each other in hoarse voices in what sounded suspiciously like German but wasn't German. Then they laughed, drew on their cigarettes and puffed smoke affectionately towards each other's faces. We wondered whether they were related – they were alike in appearance, attitude and voice, but they might have been partners, is the correct word I think, who through many years of cohabitation have come to resemble each other – perhaps met as girls at school, begun what in those days had to be a covert but was nevertheless a passionate romance, then as laws changed and the world relaxed sexually into its unhappy-go-unlucky muddle of righteousness and libertinism, came together for life as it were, finally sealing their relationship in a registry office or even a church, depending, of course, on the mores of whatever country they come from. Their unattractively united front in sneering dismissal of a gentle and courteous English couple might be a defensive habit acquired during their early years, years of wounding humiliation – on the other hand, they might merely be nasty pieces of work, lacking in manners and ordinary human decency, and now I write about them I realise that they reminded me most of all of Marge Simpson's twin sisters but without the sisters' wayward charm and sense of fun – they weren't as pretty as Marge's sisters, either, and the inert dachshund looked bogus and unpleasant, perhaps it was stuffed, or drugged, perhaps it wasn't theirs, they'd stolen it –

## Reading Matters

I'm rather puzzled by the books we've brought with us. For the first time ever we had our luggage sent ahead because I can't stand for long, my legs tend to buckle and my breathing becomes laboured. Victoria would have had a bad time keeping an eye on me as we waited for our bags to come through, and then getting them and us to the taxi and so forth. Realising that we wouldn't have to deal with our bags made us carefree in filling them, especially with books – too many of them, in fact, because I can't find any principle in my own selection, apart from the poetry, two editions of *The Oxford Book of English Verse* (Gardner and Ricks), two of *The Oxford Book of Modern Verse* (Yeats and Larkin), an edition of Hardy, selections of Wordsworth, Yeats and T. S. Eliot, all the basic stuff I yearn to have to hand on holiday, plus an edition of William Barnes, but the rest of it, the prose, seems completely arbitrary – there are even a couple of thrillers, but it's been a long time since I've been able to read a thriller, and now, now, when I feel I've got to make every book count, I can't bear the thought of reading a book that won't be helpful or appropriate. But in what way could a book be helpful or appropriate? I see that I've stuck in *The Death of Ivan Ilyich* – well, I can see how that's appropriate, but can't see how it could be helpful – in fact, its appropriateness, the story of a mediocre man coming to terms with his death, makes it far too appropriate and therefore positively unhelpful. And then there are a lot of biographies of people in whom, suddenly, I'm no longer interested – Samuel Butler, Clough, Disraeli – I think they're there because I had a plan to write a play about Florence Nightingale and simply forgot that I'd abandoned it. There are some novels by people I've heard of but never got around to reading, Musil's *The Man without Qualities*, which I've promised myself, or is it threatened myself with, since people first mentioned him at Cambridge fifty years ago. He's in three paperback volumes, is over a thousand pages altogether, and I've read about a hundred of them twice, the first time when I was in my fifties, the second time recently, in fact it was the book I was reading when I got the cancer news – I found I couldn't go on with it, I doubt if I could have gone on with any book, really, but I suspect I'd have dumped *The Man without Qualities* if I'd been in good health, it's so dazzlingly intelligent, so felinely observant, so casually erudite, and so completely static that it made me dizzy with admiration and boredom, a hundred pages and no discernible story, no glimmering of a plot, not even the feeblest narrative thrust – it's a book for patient and philosophical minds, I think, and not therefore for me – so why did I bring them, all three volumes? Oh, because I had room for them, of course. And room for *Middlemarch*. I thought it might bring comfort, as I know it so well, and there is George Eliot's voice, guiding you through her story and possibly guiding you through this time in your life when you feel such a need for wisdom and comfort. I started it last night, and didn't get far and didn't want to go further, I remembered it too well, and was afraid I wouldn't care enough, even about Lydgate, and his 'fatal spot of commonness'. So what does that leave? All these books, and not one of them, not a single one of them, attracts. Didn't I put in a novel by Stefan Zweig, with a title that reminded me of a

136

Jacobean play, *Women Beware Women*? – 'Beware' comes into it –

Yes, I've got it. *Beware of Pity*, by Stefan Zweig. Why this? Now let's think – yes, I picked it up at Daunt's partly because the cover caught my eye – I'm looking at it now – it's the Klimt of Schubert at the piano, Schubert clothed in black with an abundance of black hair and a long, thick black sideboard, but his face in profile is pink and pudgy. Beside him a woman is singing, she is young and pretty, with a halo of pink and brown air that looks like – it may even be – a hat, and beside her another young woman listens intently, with her head bowed towards perhaps a candle, perhaps a slender vase of flowers – all my perhapses and qualifications are because, though it's a charming and suggestive picture, it's slightly muzzy, and one can't tell whether that's true of the original or has been exaggerated in reproduction. Either way it's eye-catching. In fact I might well have bought the book simply for its cover, but I also wanted to find out about Stefan Zweig. His is one of those names that's always been on the periphery – I mean for me – an early twentieth-century Viennese intellectual would have been my guess, from dimly recalled and unassorted titbits, and I see from the first sentence of the tiny biography that indeed he

137

was, born in 1881, of a wealthy Austrian-Jewish family, but it doesn't say what else he wrote, how irritating, how very irritating. When did he die? Good God, he died in 1942, 'he and his wife were found dead in bed in an apparent double suicide'. What does that mean, apparent? What would the alternatives be? An accident? A murder and a suicide, either way around? Did he or they leave a note? Here's a photograph of him on the back of the bio page, taken in his late forties, his expression is pleased and eager. Long fine nose with a serious moustache under it, alert eyes, thinning hair and a high forehead. He looks very like Adolphe Menjou, who was Irish-American, I think, and Anton Walbrook, who was Viennese, I think. I really wish we had a computer with us, so that I could google Stefan Zweig. And Adolphe Menjou and Anton Walbrook, come to that. Anyway, Zweig's face on the photograph doesn't strike one as being the face of a suicide, in that it's not only 'pleased and eager', as I observed above, but it's also positively complacent, in a sympathetic way, a modest man who knows that he's famous and important. Why, then, would he commit suicide, that is if it was a real as opposed to an 'apparent' suicide? Did he have a terminal illness? Cancer? But then he wouldn't take his wife with him, just for the sake of her company,

I hope. Let's look at the bio again – oh, in Brazil, he died in Brazil – well, of course in 1942 he would have been in exile, Austria in the clutches of another Austrian. As a Jew Zweig's books would have been banned, probably burnt, his whole world in flames and about to become rubble, enough reason at sixty-two to kill himself, and his wife might have felt the same. Or, assuming that she was also Austrian, she didn't want to be a homeless widow. As soon as I get home I'll find out all about him – in the meantime I might as well read *Beware of Pity*. Try it, at least.

No, I don't think so. I think I'd really rather read poetry tonight. One of the Oxford books, the Helen Gardner for once, I've thumbed through the Ricks so often that I always seem to dip into the same pages, read the same poems again and again, all the Donne, all the Herbert, then skip to Pope's 'Letter to Arbuthnot' and the Fourth Book of *The Dunciad*, then Wordsworth's 'Immortality Ode', his poem in memory of James Hogg, some Coleridge – always 'Frost at Midnight' and 'Dejection', then occasionally something exotic and opium-driven, 'Kubla Khan' or 'The Ancient Mariner' – they're never really right for my mood, but once started they're hard to stop, on to Keats, 'Autumn', 'Nightingale' and 'Urn', ending with the fragment from 'The Fall of Hyperion – A Dream', and then nothing much until Hardy, Edward Thomas, Yeats, Eliot, really my own personal anthology, and never breaking new ground, although it's rich enough, especially when in the state I'm in now, when I don't really want to break new ground, but to be comforted by the poems that have always brought me comfort – still, I'll have a quick go at the Gardner, open it anywhere and see what happens – actually I find I've picked up the Yeats *Modern Verse*, ages since I've looked into that.

And it'll be ages until I look into it again, which means I'll never look into it again, what a disgrace of a selection, what a shabby, mean-spirited, pompous – how could a great poet have done such a thing? And the Introduction! I'd forgotten how vague, self-important and prejudiced – his dismissal of the war poets, not a poem by Owen, not a single poem, but pages of Edith Sitwell and Lascelles Abercrombie and Laurence Binyon, and Edwin John Ellis and lots of other poets with three names, William Henry Davies, Thomas Sturge Moore, George William Russell, and some of them OK, W. H. Davies for a minute or two, but none of them should be in an Oxford anthology, oh, here's one with four names, you'd expect to come across them on a tombstone – Leonard Alfred George Strong – here's this from him:

> I sweep the street and lift me hat
> As persons come and persons go,
> Me lady and me gentleman:
> I lift me hat – but you don't know!
>
> I've money by against I'm dead:
> A hearse and mourners there will be!
> And every sort of walking man
> Will stop to lift his hat to me!

Yes, that and no Owen, Rosenberg, Sassoon – and one poem by Edward Thomas, one poem! and not really a very good one, I suppose Yeats decided that Thomas was just and merely a war poet – but enough of this, your time has become precious, don't forget, and you're wasting it on bile, just remind yourself of what Yeats himself wrote, and how much of him you love to read, toss his anthology aside, and plunge into the Gardner –

I trawled along very enjoyably, profitably, I think – I opened on Marvell, which was a stroke of luck, because there they were, the ones I would have wanted, which are probably in the Ricks but I've never looked, and of course I should have – 'To His Coy Mistress', 'The Garden', 'The Definition of Love' and best of all, because I haven't read it for years and

141

years, 'The Picture of Little T.C. in a Prospect of Flowers' – and then straight into Henry Vaughan, 'The Retreat' and 'Peace' and 'The World' with that opening –

> I saw Eternity the other night,
> Like a great ring of pure and endless light,
> All calm, as it was bright

but I didn't hang about in that neighbourhood, or nip back to Donne and Herbert, I did a big jump with my eyes closed, taking an oath that I would read all the poems by whichever poet I arrived at, and almost reneged when I landed in the middle of Sir Walter Scott – the thing is that I've never been able to read his novels – I bought a whole set when I was at Cambridge, over fifty years ago, for about a pound, and they're still in my study, a whole shelf of small red books with small print and pages that cling to your fingers when you try to turn them over – I've come across articles by Alan Massie and A. N. Wilson that persuade me that Scott is a great writer, but it's no good, as soon as I pick up a volume with one hand, the other hand snatches it away and puts it back on the shelf – as for his poems, well, I always think I know them because I learned one or two at school, prep school I think, for patriotic reasons –

Breathes there the man with a soul so dead,
Who never to himself hath said,
'This is my own, my native land!'

my ten-year-old chest swelled when I recited it – my
chest hasn't swelled often since, except when I take
Casodex for my prostate, and then it's a different
swelling of my chest, into bosoms really –

and of course there was

O, young Lochinvar is come out of the west,
Through all the wide Border his steed
was the best.

and so forth, and so forth, that and a few others were
Scott's poetry for me, but I stuck to my pledge and
read through them and was pleased to do so, finding them rather thrilling, in fact, and then just
towards the end, the last poem but one and immediately after 'The Rover's Farewell' there was this,
which made my hair shift on my scalp –

*Madge Wildfire's Song*

Proud Maisie is in the wood,
    Walking so early;
Sweet Robin sits on the bush,
    Singing so rarely.

'Tell me, thou bonny bird,
    When shall I marry me?'
'When six braw gentlemen
    Kirkward shall carry ye.'

'Who makes the bridal bed,
    Birdie, say truly?'
'The grey-headed sexton
    That delves the grave duly.

'The glow-worm o'er grave and stone
    Shall light thee steady;
The owl from the steeple sing,
    Welcome, proud lady!'

## 'No!' to a Bare Bodkin, but –

– at some point, at any point, come to think of it, I can pull out – refuse radiotherapy, refuse chemotherapy, refuse to see Drs Omar, Morgan Morgan and Rootle, accept that I have a terminal illness and let it all happen as it happens. Or I can drop out when the pain becomes too much to bear – I have a low threshold when it comes to pain – 'drop out', a euphemism for kill myself, why not put it uneuphemistically – I can always kill myself as soon as I find that living is an agony, but how? is the question I've put to myself quite often over the last months, how exactly does one kill oneself in a fashion that causes the least distress to those one loves – and the least inconvenience to many people that one doesn't love, but has no right to inconvenience? I've often been infuriated by having a journey interrupted by 'a body on the line', thinking how selfish and thoughtless, and then making myself remember Anna Karenina, and the agony of despair, akin to madness, that drove her to throw herself in front of the train – also it may not be a planned act, it might be a coincidence of despair striking at a railway station, the realisation that one step, one small step – it comes hurtling along so invitingly, you'll be caught up in all that rush and noise and you'll be gone, you'll be gone, you'll be gone – I used to have the impulse at Highgate Tube Station, and had to press myself against the wall of the tunnel between the two platforms, the southbound and the northbound, although it was always the southbound train I was inclined towards, the trains that went to Camden Town, Tottenham Court Road, Waterloo, Morden – I remember that, too, whenever I'm exasperated by a body on the line – or is it 'person' they say, 'person on the line'. Or possibly 'customer' these days – 'a customer on the line'.

*

145

The fact is that I don't want to die violently, even by self-inflicted violence, it would seem more like an act of murder, and though I have serious misgivings about my character and much of my behaviour over the last seventy years, I don't hate myself enough to want to punish myself with death. I'm merely thinking of how I can escape months of pain, at the same time releasing Victoria from the burden of having to deal with it. I've seen three people die of cancer – my mother, and two of my closest friends. My mother, a tall, athletic woman with a fiery nature and a strut to her walk, even at the age of fifty-nine, became in three months so shrunken and gaunt that I couldn't bear to look at her. The doctor took pity on her and on her husband and their three sons by administering a final dose of morphine, so that she died virtually mid-hallucination –

The first friend to die of cancer was Ian Hamilton, fine poet and critic, at the age of sixty-four. He became aware that something was wrong with him on the opening night of my play *Japes*. He told me the following day that at the interval he'd gone for a piss, and out had shot a jet of blood with bits of matter mixed in it – he'd no idea it was coming, he'd felt well – in fact, never better, he'd said, and his trip to the lavatory hadn't been particularly urgent, he'd just felt that he'd better go, because it was the interval. I asked him what he thought caused it, this fount of blood instead of urine, he said he had no idea. He seemed both amused and shocked by it. He was seeing a doctor very soon, at the hospital I now go to, as a matter of fact, a woman who was presumably in the same unit or team as my lot and therefore probably quite young. She opened the interview by handing him his scan. He could make nothing of it, though he studied it carefully – he didn't really know what he should be looking at, or for, and said that it reminded him of his breakfast. She took the scan from him and said, 'You'll probably be dead in three months. Now do you think it's funny?' He escaped as soon as he could, went down to the car park and smoked a cigarette, knowing only one thing with any certainty, that he could never, under any circumstances, see that brute of a doctor again. He went to a different hospital, where the doctor, a woman, kindly and sympathetic, who wasn't offended by his attempts to find courage in jokes, took him on. It turned out that he had a tumour near his bladder, hence the jet of blood instead of urine, and he had tumours in his lungs and his liver. I don't know whether he thought smoking was a primary cause, actually I don't think he much cared, for him his cancer was a fucking nuisance, and therefore an enemy, a personal enemy – but then Ian was by nature combative, a bit of a warrior, and in his early years positively enjoyed making enemies – in his last months he was unrecognisable, only recently a sturdy and handsome man, he had been made bloated and bald by chemotherapy, in his last days he could scarcely walk or talk, though he found immense energy at the very end, his partner Patchy told me, angry and defiant and tormented, trying to heave himself up and grapple with death as if in a bar-room brawl with it.

The second friend to die of cancer was Alan Bates, fine actor and famously beautiful man. He remained beautiful to the last, and seemed not to mind the dying, he felt he'd had a successful life, and a good one – but then Alan was never ashamed of his cancer, he thought of it as possibly just a mistake on, presumably, nature's part, and he accepted it with tolerance, almost as if it weren't a personal matter. I suppose if I could die like him, serenely and for the most part painlessly – but I doubt if I would, as these things are also a matter of temperament, I suspect, and Alan was by nature amiable and conciliatory, in many of his relationships a touch passive – completely unlike Ian –

Well, what are you? Yes, what are you, what sort of death would you make, do you think? How can I answer that? I don't know, but you should try to think, shouldn't you, because surely the kind of death you imagine is in store for you will help you decide whether you kill yourself or let nature and medicine have their way. So?

## Sicko and Thicko Discuss the Origins of the Moral Sense

So?

*Well, are you by nature conciliatory or are you combative?*

Both. Generally alternately. Combative until I meet resistance, and then I become conciliatory.

*A bully and a coward, then?*

Well – yes.

*Come on, come on, admit it, admit it, you're a bully and a coward, and a coward and a bully, admit it!*

Yes yes, a coward and a bully, a bully and a coward, so please leave me alone now, please.

*I'm just getting started.*

I'm not going on with this unless you stop shouting.

*OK.*

Oh, thank you, thank you.

*Not at all, not at all. A pleasure. Now explain to me, if you would, how being a bully and a coward works in practice, in your daily life.*

Well, let me think. Yes. I'm often caught between a desire to please people and a desire to tell them the truth, so end up by doing neither.

*You equate being a bully with telling the truth and desiring to please people with cowardice?*

Presumably these basic characteristics, drives, whatever they are, manifest themselves in complicated ways in my social behaviour. Bullying and cowardice are somewhere near the murky bottom of my self.

*Somewhere near? And at the very bottom?*

Greed and fear, I assume. That's the Hobbesian view, and I've always thought it to be the right one.

*On what evidence?*

From what I feel going on in myself, and what I understand from what I observe in other people.

*So really you're saying you're only human.*

On the other hand, what a piece of work is man. I

believe that, too. Greed and fear are refined by consciousness, and further refined, until the initial impulses are disguised, and even nearly lost. So we have table manners, Mozart, Chekhov –

*And Shakespeare and so forth and so forth, eh?*

Actually, the thing about Shakespeare – the thing about him –

*Is what? What is the thing about Shakespeare?*

That he never loses touch with the initial impulses – for instance, when Hamlet forces himself to believe that he can kill, and then kills the wrong man, and then decides the wrong man will do for starters, when Macbeth finds out what it means to kill a king, and then kills him anyway, or when Lear discovers where his life is when he discovers Cordelia dead – they're almost like physical throbs, these moments of understanding. Shakespeare's above all the great poet of the particular, so in fact his greatest poetry isn't his, it belongs to Hamlet, Coriolanus, Macbeth, Lear – to this particular man at this particular moment in these particular and devastating circumstances – there are no great truths in Shakespeare that aren't wrung from the immediate, which is why you can also find their perfectly truthful opposites somewhere in his work – people are always quoting the

151

saying – all art aspires to the condition of music – but really I think that all art aspires to the condition of literature –

*Which doesn't have a universal language. Which music has.*

Yes, that's why it's an aspiration. Literature is rooted in the particularity of language. No other art has that particularity. On the other hand, all other arts can be universal, in the way that literature can't be. But an Englishman who can't read Russian or French can still have a strong sense of what Raskolnikov and Pierre, or Emma Bovary and Julian Sorel go through, while music can't give us a Raskolnikov or a Pierre or a Madame Bovary or a Julian Sorel. So even in translation there's a certain universality about literature. Some literature. Not poetry. For instance, nobody who reads Baudelaire in translation would think for a moment that he's reading great poetry.

*So really, apart from Shakespeare, you're talking about novels?*

Yes, well they touch our sympathy, the best of them, even in translation.

*Sympathy? That's an odd word, coming from a man who believes that Hobbes is right, that at our murky bottom we're composed of greed and fear.*

But I also believe that Hume is right, that we have sympathy – a faculty of sympathy.

*So what it comes down to is that your personal philosophy is an amateurish synthesis of Hobbes and Hume?*

I haven't got a personal philosophy. I'm merely using Hobbes and Hume as a way of describing my understanding of myself – of the way I've felt, of the way I've behaved –

*And this faculty of sympathy that you read about in Hume?*

It's the recognition of other people's feelings through the awareness of those feelings, or the possibility of them, in myself.

*You sympathise with other people's fear and greed because you're frightened and greedy yourself?*

That puts it very crudely.

*Yes, but then it's pretty crude.*

Sympathy, the faculty of sympathy, or the power of sympathy, seems to me a wondrous thing. It's the dove in us, according to Hume, as opposed to the serpent. Also, it's essential both for self-preservation and for the preservation of society. Every good act comes from it, as do the feelings that cause us so much distress and so – sometimes – manage to stop us from doing bad things to people, or from doing them again – sometimes.

*What feelings are those?*

Guilt, shame, remorse – you know perfectly well.

*And those come from which? Greed or fear? Or both?*

Well, fear, historically speaking. We form society because it's safer, societies depend on laws and customs for their survival, and laws and customs depend for their survival on rewards and punishments – gradually this primitive system becomes internal and increasingly complicated, our rewards come in states of consciousness, peace of mind – for instance, the satisfaction of helping others – while the punishments –

*Guilt, shame, remorse, etc.?*

Exactly. Look, I really haven't got a head for this sort of thinking. That's why I've stuck to writing plays.

*OK. Then let's get back to your own particularity, shall we? Your claim that you're a bully and a coward. Or is that just a boast?*

I wish it were, but right from childhood – well, when I went to school in Montreal at the age of six I was bullied because I was different. For one thing I still had an English accent. I was beaten up by the school gang on a daily basis. There is a gap in my memory, I don't know how I got to the next stage, but the next stage was being taken into the gang that beat me up, and being allowed to join in the beating up of other boys who were different, mainly Jews and Catholics. Eventually I became one of the beaters-up in chief. There's a very good account of the process in Sartre's *Childhood of a Leader*, about the birth of an anti-Semite.

*But you grew out of it?*

I hope so. But you never know. Things stir some-times. And like many of my generation I've never been put to the test. I thank God that I wasn't a German in 1930, for example. Or a Russian at that period. Or a dependant of a slave-trader. I'm always amazed at the ease with which people now assume – as a matter of course – that they would have rebelled against the moral norm of other times, other countries. How long did it take the abolition-ists to win over the House of Commons? Years and years and then more years. I think most MPs now are as morally supine and as greedy as the MPs then, and if you could perform some magical time switch, so that they kept their current personalities but were otherwise adjusted historically, they would have mostly voted against abolition. And if you stuck them in Hitler's Germany or Stalin's Russia you'd find them in equivalent positions to the ones they occupy here and now – promulgating race laws, scrambling for a position in the politburo. I'd like to stop this. I really don't want to spend the time I have left on anything but the life I have left.

*OK. Where were you?*

Considering whether I ought to be planning suicide.

## Will Somebody Please Tell Me Which and How Many?

The temptation will be to keep postponing it until it's too late. But choosing the right time will also depend on the how. If I rule out violence, jumping from the Clifton Suspension Bridge, throwing myself under a train, cutting my throat, thrusting a knife into my heart, and try to sort out a tranquil and painless method, I imagine I'd have to come in the end to pills. Well, I've more than thought about pills – I've been storing them ever since I got the news. Zimovane (my sleeping pills) and co-proxamol, which is an analgesic that doesn't affect the liver or the stomach. Now when Dr David Kelly, the UN inspector of weapons of mass destruction who reported on Iraq, was found sitting dead under a tree in a field, he was at first declared to have committed suicide by taking an overdose of co-proxamol and then slitting his wrists, and I remember even then, long before the discovery of my cancer, that this was useful information to have about co-proxamol, should the need ever arise etc., but later it came out that he'd vomited up most of the co-proxamol un-digested and that a number of experts, medical experts I assume, claimed that there wasn't enough left in his system to have killed him, nor had he lost enough blood to cause his death, and recently there have been rumours that he was murdered. This is depressing for many reasons, among them my own personal reason – as I've said, I've no intention of cutting my wrists, the thought of it makes them tin-gle with dread – but I had hoped that co-proxamol was a sure thing. Now I have to accept the possibil-ity that I'd just vomit the pills up. Also I have no idea how many you'd have to keep down to do the job. I suppose if I washed down say fifteen with a bottle of Scotch, the Scotch might help to absorb them into my system. On the other hand, I'm not sure I could drink a bottle of Scotch, or even a glass of it, or even a teaspoonful – I've come to loathe the smell of alcohol. There's an irony to be foraged out of this, I think, that I gave up alcohol because it was killing me, and now that I want to kill myself I can't take it up again. Well, what about the sleepers, zimovane? I've been taking them for years and they seem jolly effective – one generally puts me out, and on occasional bad nights two will do the trick. Of course they're much helped in their work by Victoria, who always puts her arms around me shortly after I come to bed, the combination is so soothing, so lulling. But I can't ask Victoria to put her arms around me when I've taken an overdose, she might find herself charged with a criminal offence, assisting with a suicide possibly, so I'll have to rely on the zimovane alone. But how many? And actually, are they the right sort of sleeping pills? You hear and read stories of people who've gobbled down bottles of sedatives but instead of dying they turn into vegetables – whenever I hear or read that phrase, 'he turned into a vegetable', I always think of a marrow or a cucumber. Well, it would be awful if I turned into a cucumber or a marrow, and Victoria had to tend me – watering me, cleaning me, and settling me down – although in reality I would just be an inert lump, with tubes sticking out of me, my chest rising and falling with mechanical regularity. She couldn't grieve over me because there I would be, technically alive, a drain on her emotions and eventually her health.

So really, yes, it's a bit of a problem. It's one thing to see coolly the need to kill myself at some point in my dying, quite another thing to work out how to do it. The obvious person to provide information would be a doctor, but there's doubtless some code of professional ethics that would prevent him from spilling the beans. I could try to pretend that I'm writing a thriller, 'There's a chap I want to knock off at the end, it's got to look like a suicide, what would be the best sleeping pill, would zimovane do it, and how many precisely?' but would he believe me? If I found the right doctor he could pretend to believe me. Well, for the moment all I can do is make sure that I always have a lot of co-proxamol and zimovane to hand, and hope that someone will turn up who'll give me the right information. And when I've got that sorted out, I'll have to work out where, and at what time of the day or night, so that nobody is inconvenienced or embarrassed, and so that it is in some way supportable for Victoria. I'll want her by me, and she's said she wants to be by me, right up to the end, but I can only let her in so far as it's legally possible.

# A Night on the Town and Afterwards

We took a taxi into Agios Nikolaus for dinner this evening. We stopped at a Vodafone place to see if we could get the BlackBerry to work, but a rather indolent and ill-tempered girl said they could do nothing with it, the signals had been set wrong for Greece, which didn't make sense as we'd used it in Spetses last year. The owner of the shop, or perhaps he was the manager, came out from the back, and took a politer and more concerned view. He opened the BlackBerry up, made a phone call which lasted a long time and caused him to smile and laugh often – the taxi ticking away through all this – then hung up, closed the BlackBerry and handed it back, saying there was nothing they could do, the signals were set wrong for Greece. We returned to the taxi and asked to be taken to the nearest supermarket, as I needed to stock up on white chocolate, to which I'm addicted – in fact, I can't get to sleep unless I've gulped down at least half a bar of a large Green & Black's. It was a strangely tortuous and complicated journey, from the Vodafone place in the centre of town to the outskirts. The supermarket was as ghastly as our local Tesco's in London, but less busy, not at all busy. Actually, we were virtually the only customers, so it had a mortuary feel to it – and at least our local Tesco's sold Green & Black's white chocolate. This supermarket didn't sell any white chocolate at all. I had to make do with milk chocolate, which usually makes me feel sick and gives me a headache. I bought ten bars of it – enough to last me, I hope – then back to the taxi. We asked to be taken to the lake, where the young man at reception had told us there were many restaurants, and indeed there were many, many restaurants. We walked along, peering into them, not seeing much difference between them in the seating arrangements, and not much difference in the menus, large versions of which were posted outside, with photographs of the dishes on offer. The lurid colours of heaps of bright red spaghetti and scarlet crabs and violent green salads and corpse-white squares of feta cheese made the food look disgusting, and when we turned away from it we invariably found ourselves facing the – I don't know what he was – maître d' doesn't sound right, but he was more than just a waiter – he was a sort of pimp, actually, he was pimping his restaurant, 'Allo, yas, good ivnin, lovely and licious plates ere, you like, you come in, yas, come in,' and when we smiled apologetically and moved off, he would shout after us, 'Tankyewverraverramush, sir, ma-

dame, tankyewverraverramush,' not sarcastically
but mechanically, and the thing was these pimps all
looked the same, short and burly, unshaven, in
baggy grey trousers and messy white shirts, though
one or two had stained white and blue aprons, but
they all had the same blank eyes, never looking at
you even when they described in an intimate voice
the specialities of the house.

In the end we sat down at a table that was more
on the pavement than in the restaurant, not that we
chose it but the pimp was broader and fatter than his
rivals, and instead of following us with invitations in
a fairly loud voice and then dropping away to track
another client, he stepped in front of us and spoke in
a low, insinuating murmur, which made him sound
more salacious than the others, indeed slightly per-
verted, as if he were at the gastro-paedophile end of
the market, and he also extended his arm. It could
have been a conversational gesture, but it prevented
us from walking deafly ahead. Trudging politely
around him, we also crossed the line, so to speak, into
his establishment, which began at the edge of the
pavement. He pulled a chair out for Victoria, who hes-
itated, we shrugged at each other and sat down. There
was no doubt that it was a lively position – all nationalities, English, Welsh and Scottish, passed by in what
frequently looked like the costumes of their countries,

the Scotidge were dumpy men in tartan shorts and shirts, the dumpy men in nursery jumpsuits I took to be the Welsh. The English wore a combination of the infantile and the threatening – cut-off trousers with chains looping out of the pockets and shirts that had no sleeves but were tattered at the shoulder, as if they'd been ripped in a drunken rage, although were no doubt sold that way, and were probably expensive – these were the young men, and mainly the young women, but the middle-aged and elderly were merely inelegant and dowdy, the women in unbecoming tracksuits and shapeless dresses or – if they were fat – shorts and T-shirts with slogans on them. In all of them, whatever their age and costume, was an innate courtesy that made it impossible for them to get past the pimps without apologising, explaining that they'd eaten already or were going to meet friends or – in one case, a North Country couple in their sixties – that they were still recovering from a bit of stomach trouble they'd picked up the other night, but tomorrow they hoped to be over it and they would certainly like to try this restaurant, as it wasn't the restaurant that had caused the trouble, it was one a little further down – the pimp patted them both on the arm without looking at them, 'Tankyewverramush,' he said, 'tankyewverraverramush,' and as the couple went off they gave each other a grin, so they'd obviously delivered a prepared alibi – there were other nationalities, of course, French, Dutch, German, and the pimps were presumably saying in their language the sort of thing they said in ours. There were also groups and couples of Chinese and Japanese – I think this is the first time I've ever seen Chinese and Japanese in Greece – the Japanese stood politely listening to the pimps, and asked questions in English, while the Chinese, I suppose more used to the huckstering and pimp approach, went past with fixed smiles, or took photographs, which our particular pimp actually posed for, beside his menu, then watched them turn into the next restaurant and sit down – watched, I might say, without rancour.

The lake is small – more like an enormous puddle – but it has a few ducks on it, and a few rowing boats also, and then there are the lights reflected in the water, and the sounds drifting across from the other side, all the bustle and animation. It was fun sitting there, and remained fun even when the food arrived. But then you don't come to Greece for the food, just as you don't come to England for the people –

A toothsome, high-breasted but slightly grubby waitress cleared the overflowing plates away and we paid the bill – preposterously cheap when you consider how much had been put in front of us, preposterously expensive when you consider how little we'd been able to eat – and strolled off, the pimp's farewell 'Tankyewverramush' soiling our ears. We went around the lake and up one of the very busy streets, looking into the shop windows. They were full of luxury goods, fashionable underwear, expensive watches. One had shelves on shelves of cigarettes, it was called Tobacco Warehouse. It was like any street now, I suppose, in any European tourist town. We couldn't see shops selling specifically Greek things, but what are specifically Greek things, things you'd want to buy because they were made in Greece, by Greeks? I can't think of a single thing that you look forward to buying in Greece, except cheap cigarettes.

As we strolled along I began to feel that oddness, when all energy goes out of me, just like that, my legs begin to buckle. I had to catch Victoria's arm and cling to her to stay upright. The taxi driver who'd brought us in had dropped us close to a rank, so we knew where to go. It wasn't far, no more than fifty yards or so, but I couldn't make it, and sank on to a café chair on the pavement, feeling on the edge of consciousness, my legs watery, my breathing short and abrupt. The lump on my neck was throbbing. I kept plucking at it, and then stroking it, to soothe it. Victoria ordered a couple of espressos, and we sat with her hand on mine. When the coffee came

I had trouble lifting the cup to my lips, but managed a sip, and it was delicious – the most delicious taste since we came to Greece. I began to feel better, whether it was the wonderful espresso or the resting, I don't know, but some energy and strength came back. I tried to explain what had happened and how it felt – the question really being, was it the work of the cancer or of the radiotherapy, the illness or the treatment? If the latter, then perhaps these collapses are actually good signs –

Back at the hotel, we looked in at the bar for another coffee. It was full of English and Scottish, noisy and mostly drunk, not nasty drunk but jolly and singsongy and laughter-at-the-top-of-the-voice drunk. There was a man playing something that looked like a piano but was actually one of those music machines that produce all kinds of instrumental effects, organ, violin, flute, trumpet – when we went in he was producing a combination of them, and singing loudly enough to be heard over the din. The room stank of cigarette smoke and I realised that I'd come to loathe all cigarette smoke except my own – but then one doesn't smell one's own cigarette smoke, or not in the way that one smells other people's.

We went out on to the terrace, where there was only one other couple, young, English and elegant, she blonde and pretty, in a shimmering silver skirt, and he dark and handsome in a pouty and ill-tempered sort of way. He was talking into his mobile, breaking off to snarl something to the woman, who would avert her head contemptuously. They were in the middle of a row, obviously, that had nothing to do with the conversation on the mobile. Their voices were too low for me to hear, though I tried, but I imagined, of course – the two of them coming to the rancorous end of an affair, perhaps one of them married but they both looked too – what? – childish? unused? to have a husband or wife somewhere – so an office romance, I guessed, a couple of moneymaking high-flyers, hedge-funders and such. If so, it would be ugly when they got back, lawsuits and harassment charges etc. Suddenly he raised his voice and said, 'So now you go to bed, darling, and here's Mummy to say goodnight,' and passed her the mobile, and she said, one could tell from her expression though not actually hear, all kinds of sweet and loving things. When she'd finished, she handed him the mobile, he tucked it into his shirt pocket and sat with his hands behind his head, sealed off, oblivious, and she sat in that way that women do, hunched and her arms crossed, hands tucked into the armpits, as if it were cold, which of course it wasn't. Then he said something, she said something, he looked at her, she laughed, he laughed and put his hand on her knee, and lit a cigarette, which they shared. So that was all right then. When we got up to leave, after a feeble, virtually caffeine-free coffee, they suddenly noticed us, she smiled prettily but he scowled, which made him look prepubescent, and as if he thought we were interlopers or eavesdroppers, for God's sake!

Now I'm sitting on the patio beside our swimming pool, there's no moon, and it's dark beyond the pool. I can't see the sea between the rocks, in fact I can't distinguish the rocks from the darkness, and I'm getting jittery, the walls-closing-in experience, not as bad as previously, but it's unsettling, and makes me think about my collapse this evening, which hasn't become a memory so much as an apprehension – It's – what is it? Nearly 3 a.m., I think I've got to get away from here, I'm too awake to go to bed, I'll go for a walk, slip out without telling Victoria, she'd worry – the key, make sure you've got your key.

I'm back. I walked along the dimly lit paths to the chapel where I sit in the daytime, and sat there, with my back against the wall, listening to the sea, its steady lapping. There were no other sounds at all, no lights in the rooms or buildings. The hotel was like a dormant town, and I would say peaceful, but I wasn't at peace, I was trying too hard, I expect, telling myself that here, in this still Cretan night, I could think awhile, accept my condition as the common condition of all living things, but my eyes were darting about, locating the bushes that I knew were there, and my ears were straining, and suddenly there came from the beach a man's laugh, clear and cruel, and a yelp, a boy's or a woman's, then another yelp and the sound of scampering and a man's voice again, this time low, urgent and angry. I got up and walked back along the paths, not running exactly, because I'm not capable of it, but at speed, swaying a bit and stumbling. I had a difficult time with the door, which jammed, as it often does, and I had pretty well to kick it down to get in. I made a dreadful din, and expected to find Victoria sitting up in shock, clutching a sheet to her breasts, as on the cover of those books I used to love, but she was deeply asleep on her side, her glasses on the tip of her nose, her book in her hand. I slipped her glasses off, which involved tilting her head a bit, took the book from her hand, put it on the table beside her bed. She mumbled something, burrowed under the sheet, and I'm here, on the patio, with a sleeping pill and two co-proxamol inside me and *The Oxford Book of English Verse* – Christopher Ricks edition – I feel

OK about the walls now, which is the main thing, at least tonight.

## A Disgusting New Habit

The newspapers come at around midday. *The Times*, the *Telegraph* and the *Guardian*, but we don't look at them until we have lunch in a café above the beach. It has a marvellous setting, the sea directly below and the mountains unfolding in the distance. Every lunchtime, though, it's a slightly different view, sometimes range after range of mountains, as far as the eye can see, sometimes just the nearest range and then clouds beyond, through which a tip rises. It would be a perfect place for lunch, with that view and comfortable chairs and efficient service, but it's ruined by the dreadful music, which is played full blast, and by the foulness of the food – enormous hamburgers with meat the texture of chewing gum, and club sandwiches you can hardly lift, let alone fit into your mouth, and when you manage a bite it takes a very long time, especially if you have teeth like mine, to convert it into swallowable pulp, which is of course quite tasteless except for a slight flavour of dust. Victoria says the salads are OK but I can't eat lettuce or greens or any of that stuff – it's not quite an allergy I have, but it's a strong aversion – but the point about the lunch is not the food, it's the newspapers, and more precisely, for me it's the obituaries.

It began in London, this new habit of turning to the obituaries first and then reading them all the way through, whether I knew the deceased or know of them or know nothing about them, going through them very quickly first of all to find out how they died, with an eye open for cancer and most particularly lung cancer – just occasionally you're not told, apart from 'died at home after a short/long illness', which always gives the impression that whether it was long or short it was the kind of illness the nearest and dearest don't want people to know he or she died of – but what I'm most interested in is how long? how long did they live, these painters, politicians, actors, sailors, soldiers, civil servants, headmasters, criminals, television presenters? how many years did they manage? If they died at seventy or under I feel a little surge of uplift, joy really, as if I'd beaten them in some tournament. But if they got beyond seventy-one I feel an envy and bitterness at the unfairness of it, and we're always told – or so it seems to me – that those who persisted to a great age did so with grace and style and full of energy, still climbing mountains at eighty-three, conducting symphonies at ninety-one, full of mirth at 106 – I think, what right did they have? who decides these things? the injustice of it! and go back to look at the piece on someone who went in his fifties, feeling not only triumph on my own account, but sympathy and indignation on his or her account. Actually I mind much less about women living longer, feeling that they have a natural and moral claim on extra years. I'm glad to note that I am distressed when I read of anyone cut down unduly young, I manage not to compare their term with mine, and feel that I have a kinship with them, especially if they knew that they were dying, and I feel sad and angry for their families. Quite a pleasant feeling, in a way, that's the awful thing.

I've tried to stop doing this, tried going first to the sports pages, as I always used to do, then to the editorials and letters, but it's no good, I can't stop, I can only delay, and so when I finally get to the obituaries my reactions have been sharpened by self-restraint and impatience, and I find myself almost gloating at the account of well, for instance, in today's – a distinguished City accountant and a gardening expert, one who made it to sixty-eight and the other who got to seventy – Christ, look at my vocabulary, 'made it to' and 'got to', yes, exactly as if they were competing, as if we're all competing, and not in terms of contribution, not how did he spend his years? what did he give to the world? how good a man was he? but for how long, for how many years?

And actually it's worse than this, my new habit or addiction. I find myself doing it almost automatically when I come across any mention of a life in the newspapers or a book blurb. I count the years between the date of birth and the date of death, usually getting very muddled, as I'm poor at mental arithmetic, but I keep at it, checking and checking again until I've established whether I'll outlive them or not. Whether I'll outlive the dead, in fact, would be the grotesque but accurate way of putting it – as I did with Stefan Zweig the other night, when studying that tiny bio. Born in 1881, died in 1942. So he would have been twenty-nine in 1900, add forty-two to twenty-nine comes to – comes to seventy-one, well, that's all right, look again, no, no, sixty-one, killed himself when he was sixty-one, that's more than all right! On the other hand, does the fact that he killed himself alter the statistics, he exercised a choice after all – but you're thinking of exercising a choice – yes, but it's a choice that's been forced on me, I'll only be lopping off a few months, Zweig might have pulled off another fifteen or twenty-nine – 'pulled off' – Christ!

I wonder if he left a letter, that's one of the first things I'm going to do when I get home, google him and find out all that I can, because now I'm into

*Beware of Pity*, I want to know everything there is to know about its author. It's a quite astonishing novel, unique, I think, in what it undertakes, which is pretty well declared in the title – well, I'm only halfway through, but how grateful I am for the impulse in Daunt's that made me pick it up, it's already crammed a lot of life into a few hours of reading – so here's to you, Stefan Zweig, long life to you!

I was just thinking – apropos my current obsession with obituaries and the length of people's lives – that I don't feel pleased that people close to me died before me and had shorter lives – Alan at sixty-nine, Ian Hamilton and Ian MacKillop and Roger Gard in their early to mid-sixties, Clive Goodwin before he was fifty, my younger brother Piers at forty-nine, James Hammerstein at sixty-seven, my mother at fifty-nine – and nor do I feel bitter and envious that others who are older than me will probably outlive me, but that's because I miss the first lot so much, and need the second lot so much, a matter of selfishness, then, triumphing over competitiveness. Or possibly the idea that you leave some part of you behind with the survivors and so have a – what? a form of afterlife in this world that is not actually you, and can't be appreciated by you, but is an idea of you that will last as long as they last.

And with luck somebody now and then might put on one of my plays or pick up one of my books, and will hear my voice, which is a consoling thought as I write it down. But will it be a consolation after I'm dead? is the real question, and the answer is obvious, so it stops being a consolation now. But at least I'll be in a true democracy for the first time in my life, where no one is more equal than anyone else – though you never know.

Actually I do feel bitter and envious that my father will have lived longer – he died at seventy-six – perhaps because I feel he had a paternal duty to make sure that I had more than he had, or perhaps because ours was an uneasy relationship, I think neither of us knew what he wanted or hoped for from the other, he depending on his wife and I on my mother to point the way – 'Your father loves you, he may be quiet and shy about it, but never forget that!' she would say to me, and sometimes, possibly, she said much the same to him – 'Simon loves you, you know, James, he may be sneering and conceited when he's with you, but in his heart he adores and admires you, James, I hope you know that!'

And there is this: that my older brother, sixteen months older brother, Nigel, died at seventy-two, just before I was told about my cancer, which left me almost no time to grieve for him before I began to grieve for myself, it seemed to be intertwined grieving, but then I've always felt that, in spite of our differences in temperament, our fates were in large matters also intertwined. He died a week before his birthday, in June. Would it be optimistic to suppose that I might be allowed until around my next birthday, thus keeping to the sixteen months of separation? It's asking for a few months more than Dr Rootle predicted, but he may not be infallible, at least to the month.

## A Great Adventure

It was very windy today, so after lunch we decided to drive towards the town, as I thought I'd glimpsed a beach or two along the way, and about halfway between the hotel and Agios Nikolaus there was indeed a beach, the public beach, so we drove into the parking area, which was both neatly organised and commodious – what does that mean, commodious? Well, I think I merely mean that though there were a lot of cars we found a space to park in quite easily. There was none of the usual rubbish you see lying about in a parking area in England. Furthermore the beach was clean, even though it was crowded – people on sunbeds, sprawled on towels, horsing about with balls and Frisbees, the atmosphere jolly and pleasant. The sand was soft, the kind you can shake off once your feet are dry, and the sea was clean, shallow enough for children to play in quite a long way out, and then deep enough to have a proper swim. There was an elegant little café on stilts, where Victoria sat and read while I went off for a stroll along the promenade.

I went quite a long way, past cafés and restaurants, noting that the sea got deeper and deeper. There were cement squares from which you could dive straight in and a ladder to climb down. I was thinking how delightful it all was when I suddenly began to feel hot, too hot, and a bit dizzy and realised that I ought to get back to Victoria in the café and the shade but couldn't face the walk. I wondered whether I had the nerve to swim. I thought I probably hadn't the energy and strength, and therefore hadn't the nerve, and then I thought, well, what the hell, what the hell, went to some nearby steps, and climbed down into the sea, which was cool and refreshing.

I took it very slowly, very gently, on my side, leisurely strokes on my side, thinking that I could always turn back to the ladder, until suddenly it was too late, I was as far from the ladder as from the beach. There was nothing for it but to toil on, to assume a calm and easy air, turning my arm over languidly, as if really I were idling along on my side, but my stroke was getting feebler and my legs kept dropping under me, to the vertical – getting them up again was becoming a conscious and laborious act, but still I was all right, making sure that my breathing was steady and regular, strolling, strolling along in the water, not panicking. A middle-aged couple walking arm in arm along the path stopped, and looked down at me. What did they see? A brave and classy swimmer making his smooth if leisurely way towards a possibly glamorous destination, or an elderly fool of a man labouring out of his depth, with a certain look in his eyes that could be identified as fear, or even as a plea. The man said something to the woman and they hurried on – and who could blame them? if they'd asked me whether I was all right I might have said, 'No, no, please help me, I can't go on much longer,' and then what could they have done? I suspect that if the positions had been reversed I'd have done what they did.

And of course if the positions had been literally reversed there'd have been two of them in the water and only one of me on land, so I would most certainly have hurried off, unseeing and deaf, leaving them to their own devices and fates. I imagined them clinging to each other and either bawling for help or wrestling each other to their deaths, possibly both, first bawling and then drowning, they'd looked attached to each other, husband and wife walking arm in arm, perhaps they'd be happy to drown arm in arm, or even better in a close embrace – a good way to go, though probably several decades earlier than they'd wish. I rolled on my back and looked up at the sky, letting my body drift, drift, and sort of knew that I was drifting, drifting away from shore, out to sea, there was a slight tightening in one of my calves, from cramp, and so the first stirrings of real panic. I let myself hang loosely so that I was atilt, my head above water, my body trailing out under it but comfortable, floating, drifting, the pain eased in my calf, and I had that feeling I have sometimes in the sea of wanting to go on drifting and on, until I drift far away, finally drifting underwater without noticing a change, simply a slipping out of two elements into one, seeping into the sea, scarcely a death, really, and so much better, so much better than rotting in bed like Freud, for instance – at the end his mouth stank so much of cancer that his dog wouldn't go near him – so much better than that sort of death, but I couldn't, not now, leaving Victoria reading in the café, alone in Crete, having to arrange to take my body back if it washed ashore, or waiting weeks for me to turn up, wrapped in seaweed, what was left of me, after the fish had had their fill – and so forth the thoughts rolled, as I lay tilted upwards in the water, with the sun beating down on my head, and without planning it I began to haul myself back towards shore, and then towards the beach, arm over, arm over, arm over, la la la, la la – I had a bit of difficulty with the cement jetty that stuck out at the end of the promenade, and had to swim out again to get around it, and then I was among people, first of all the grown-ups in singles or in pairs, then mothers and fathers playing with their children and teaching them to swim or dunking the babies, and then I was on the beach – almost the most difficult part, getting to my feet and wading to the shore. I plodded across the hot sand, around recumbent young couples who were holding hands with their faces turned towards each other, went into one of the dressing rooms, sat on the bench in a collapse, went really into a sort of coma for a while. At last it occurred to me that I'd been gone quite a long time, Victoria might have begun to worry. As I picked my way across the sand, I was actually rather proud of myself. I climbed the steps to the café and saw Victoria standing up at the table, the book in her hand, staring anxiously along the promenade. I wanted to boast – 'I've walked and then I swam for, oh, miles and miles –' though I hadn't, more like half a mile each way, well, perhaps half a mile altogether. Anyway, I didn't say anything other than 'I'm back.' 'Where have you been?' 'Oh, walked along the path a bit, went in for a dip –' I picked up a towel and went off to shower and change, and then we had lunch there, Victoria a health-giving salad and I multiple layers of bread with nothing identifiable between them, but it was pleasant, shady and peaceful, lots to look at on the beach, and no music – no music, so who cared what was in the sandwich?

On our way back we stopped out of curiosity at a hotel that we suspected might be rather grand behind its dowdy front, and indeed it was grand, the lobby spacious and cool, with a long reception counter, comfortable-looking armchairs and sofas, a bar off, and in front open glass doors through which we sauntered with the casual aplomb of paid-up guests into an enormous and jungly garden which had little white cottages scattered about in it. We went down one of the paths that led to a large lawn and the sea, and a tree-shaded walk with ladders into the water, and at intervals small beaches. We settled on one of the beaches and went for a swim. Really, it was more like a paddle than a swim, and it would have been perfect if I hadn't made a hash of trying to change discreetly, caught my foot in my trunks as

I was stepping out of them and toppled over. Victoria had to hold a towel up while I got into my trousers, protecting the people on the beach from a sight of my naked front, but exposing to the people on the lawn a distasteful view of my buttocks. Actually, I haven't seen my buttocks for ages, they might be rounded and muscular, for all I know, the buttocks of a bullfighter, for instance – well, an ex-bullfighter.

In fact, nobody paid us the slightest attention, there appeared to be no security whatsoever, there'd been no cameras in the lobby and there were none peeking out of the foliage or sticking out of the sea, and nobody walked about in police-type clothing. We realised the same was true of our own hotel – it seems to me wonderfully relaxed and typically Greek, until somebody gets mugged or murdered, of course, when it will seem to me shockingly negligent and typically Greek.

By the time we got back it was early evening, the sun was still strong and the wind had dropped. We went to our room by way of the beach, and on impulse, without really discussing it, went in for a swim, a sedate and careful swim in my case, no further out than my chest.

It's now getting on for 2 a.m., I've been writing away ever since we got back from dinner. I'm tired but it's a tiredness that is actually a pleasure, unlike the tiredness that attacks me without warning during the day, when I feel as if the blood is draining out of my soul. Here, now, as I write this, it seems impossible that I'm dying, at least until I feel the lump on my neck, which I am now doing. They said in the radiotherapy place that it would shrink after treatment, but to my fingers it's still the same size, the size of a walnut. Perhaps it's softening a bit, perhaps just a bit, but I'm not sure. I wish, I do wish, that I could stop myself fingering it. The problem is that I'm acutely conscious of it, even when it's not throbbing or tingling, and I'm sensitive to its visibility, especially on the beach, where I've noticed a couple of other people with very similar lumps on their necks – a lean hawk-like German of about my age, and a fraught English woman who is an exploited grandmother, I think – she screams anxiously to her two grandchildren, a boy and a girl of twelve, thirteen, that sort of age, warning them not to swim out so far, to come in where she can see them – then she sits smoking with a book on her lap, but her eyes are drawn to the children, and she's back on her feet, then forcing herself to sit down – well, my point is that I don't notice anyone else noticing her lump, which is closer to the ear than mine is, and I think a bit larger, or the lean hawk-like German's, which is exactly where mine is, and looks roughly the same sort of size, so I tell myself that therefore nobody notices mine, or wouldn't do if I could stop touching it. Which I will now do, and smoke a cigarette instead. The real point, the important point, is that it's been a lovely day, an adventurous one, and we've been happy, the two of us. How good that we came to Crete.

## Ghosts and Exiles

We went for a spin this afternoon, late afternoon, motored along the coast road with no particular destination in mind, although we thought we might get as far as Elounda, and have a drink there, but were through it and past it before we noticed it, and went through a couple of smaller towns until we got to Plaka, which is where the road ended. Plaka, and after Plaka nowhere, as far as we could make out. So we stopped there, just on the edge of the town, in an empty car park on the edge of the sea. It was getting on for six o'clock, the light beginning to thin, the air to cool, and before we'd got to the centre a brisk wind had sprung out of nowhere, as if it had been waiting for us to turn up. We passed a little group of three, three women who looked English and as if

184

they taught courses in discrimination awareness and gender disability, that sort of thing. They were all three of them short and slightly bulky, with hair – grey, grey, brown – cut short and they had worried, kindly expressions. As we went by they nodded and smiled and so did we. I thought I recognised one of them, and also thought I saw a glimmer of recognition in her eyes, and when I looked back she was looking back – 'Do you think we might have come across them before, one of them anyway, the one at the end?' Victoria said yes, not just the one at the end, but all three of them. We puzzled at it for a while, offering each other different contexts, mainly from our teaching days at Queen Mary College, and then agreed that they were probably a genre, so to speak, we'd met dozens like them in all sorts of contexts – in fact walking down Holland Park Avenue to two of the most serious shops in London, Daunt's bookshop and its neighbour Lidgate the butcher – you could easily imagine them coming out of Lidgate with their organic sausages and wheeling straight into Daunt's for the latest pamphlet on Jane Austen and the abolition of the slave trade.

The reason we talked about them so much, also speculating on where they were staying in Plaka, was because they'd turned off a path that seemed to lead towards a field, then rough countryside and eventually the mountains, and they hadn't been dressed for adventure, nor were they built for it, nor did they seem inclined to it, so where were they going? The other reason we talked about them was because they were the only people we saw in Plaka until we reached the centre of town, where there appeared to be no tourists or visitors but ourselves, and the few natives that were visible were silent. They were hanging out washing or sweeping the fronts of their houses and cafés, mainly they were middle-aged women, within easy speaking distance of each other, some of them, but not speaking, as if they were so used to each other they were no longer aware that they were there.

We went along the main street, which consisted of the usual Greek seaside shops, selling the usual seaside things, there was a small supermarket and several electrical shops and so forth. Outside most of these shops the owner or manager was standing smoking, or sitting in a chair smoking or reading a paper or with his hands on his knees. They were all men, of different ages, and apart from them the street was empty – again, not a single tourist, not a single customer on the street, only the two of us walking along it and making a point of not glancing into the windows and arousing expectations – but none of them looked as if they believed or hoped we might go in and make a purchase, they looked as if, to all intents and purposes, their shops were closed and they were only sitting or standing in front of them because they had nothing else to do, nowhere else to go.

There was only one other proper street in Plaka, it met the main street at a crossroads, and then did a little loop and ran along the side of the beach. It stretched for about a hundred yards and on both sides there were restaurants, and only restaurants, right next to each other and sometimes seeming to overlap into each other, so you couldn't tell where one ended and the other began. They had outside them large menus with photographs, as in the restaurants beside the lake in Agios Nikolaus, and also, as by the lake in Agios Nikolaus, a man outside, pimping. But there was none of the ebullience, the hectoring and imploring, of Agios Nikolaus – hardly surprising, I suppose, as again we were the only other people on the street. It was grim and slightly unnerving walking down it, right in the middle of the street, and only just hearing from our left and our right low murmurs in English offering us lamb, chicken, pasta, salads, fresh fish. There was no belief in their voices, no enthusiasm, actually no real interest, and there were no customers inside, not one table in all these restaurants was occupied, and there seemed to be no staff either. We scarcely dared raise our eyes, from embarrassment or even a kind of shame, we seemed to be intruding on a display of failure and defeat. It was a relief to get to the end and walk along the promenade. The sea was grey and miserable, the wind was now quite cutting, altogether it was such an unexpected and eerie experience – well, spooky, actually, and depressing – the grey hostile sea and the sense that we'd just walked through a ghost town, even the shop-owners and the restaurateurs were like ghosts, as if they weren't real even to themselves. We were getting cold, but just as we were about to turn back we came to a quay and a sign in English giving the times of the ferry to Spinalonga, the small island which had been used for a leper colony in the first half of the twentieth century. I knew a little about it from a marvellous book on leprosy by my old and dear friend Tony Gould, and Victoria had a fresher knowledge, having read not only Tony's book, but a recent and successful novel called *The Island* set in Plaka and Spinalonga. We stared across at the island, which was huddled in dreariness just a short boat ride away, and said well, we must come back on a warmer day and look at the little town where the lepers had lived out their lives, see their homes, their shops and their restaurants and imagine what it was like to have been carried across this short stretch of sea to your final home, everyone in your life now a leper like yourself. From its shore you'd be able to see the healthy mainland, people moving about their business and their pleasure. Yes, we must certainly come back and make the trip, we said, as we hurried to the car and drove away, we really must, perhaps in a couple of days, put aside a whole afternoon before we go home, make a proper outing of it – but I think we both knew we wouldn't, we'd seen something of Plaka when nobody else was looking and that was quite enough.

On the way back we stopped at Elounda, a charming little town, lively and colourful and full of luxury-goods shops, among them a shop that sells Canadian fur coats at low prices – there was one in the window, at what seemed a very high price to me, but how odd to think of someone buying a fur coat in a tourist town in Crete. Do they wear it through customs and immigration, to avoid paying duty, or do Greeks buy them, does it get that cold in Athens in winter that you'd wear a Canadian fur coat?

We didn't stay long in Elounda as I had one of those near-fainting episodes, just managed to get back to the car. As soon as we were in our room I went to bed, and slept. I'm all right again now, in a moment I'll dip into Larkin's Oxford anthology and smoke one, perhaps two, I hope not three cigarettes.

## If You Can't See Her Legs, Don't Ask Her for a Dance

I haven't so much as looked at this pad recently, not at night, when I've been on the patio, nor during the day, when I've been at my usual place – at the table with my back against the chapel wall. They've been beautiful days, and I would like to have written that down about each of them. We've been going to the hotel down the road, with the lawns and the marvellous water you can ladder down into or walk gently into from one of their beaches – very good lunches in a delightful restaurant that overlooks the bay, hot and cold buffets or a mixture of both with not much Greek stuff in it apart from stuffed peppers and such. We have a swim before lunch, and a swim after lunch – they have showers and changing rooms, everything you need – and then back to the hotel in the late afternoon for another swim. Sometimes we go back to the other hotel for dinner. And sometimes we eat here, at the restaurant by the chapel or the swanky restaurant with tables around the swimming pool where there's a small band and a middle-aged male singer – he has an OK voice with sad eyes and a smarmy delivery. There is also a young female singer – she has a lousy voice that sets your teeth on edge. She likes to sway and screech on the edge of the pool, and so interferes with your meal as you keep watching her in the hope that she'll fall in. A few of the guests dance, mostly the elderly ones, and they're really rather good, with complicated steps and twirls, the ladies in long dresses, high heels, necklaces, earrings, the men in short-sleeved shirts and loose trousers. The other night there was a man in canvas shorts and a see-through shirt. He was small and burly, with no hair on his chest, like me, and with a chubby, rather sweet face – what you could see of it behind his large sunglasses, the ones that look like wings – and he was wearing shiny black shoes, his dancing pumps, I suppose. His wife was taller by some inches, handsome with a mass of grey hair piled up, a pearl choker and a long, trailing dark red gown, the whole effect of her fine and Edwardian. They made an eccentric-looking couple, though they danced well, he particularly, he was properly dominating, swinging her about and making her crouch to run under his arm and then he twirled her. I'd like to have seen them do something racy and dangerous, one of those homicidal Spanish or South American numbers.

191

So that's all we've been doing in the last few days. For many hours together I've almost forgotten about the cancer and the prognosis. It's there only as a faint stain on my consciousness except at night, when it becomes more than that, but there seems no point in writing that down. The great thing is that if I turn to Stefan Zweig's *Beware of Pity* I can escape for as long as I'm reading it, which is why I've been going so slowly. Also it's too good to read except with the closest attention, and so painful that I have to put it down constantly.

The story is really very simple. Anton Hofmiller, an Austrian cavalry officer stationed in a remote garrison town in the months before the First World War, goes one evening to a party given by the richest landowner in the area, a widower. He has a splendid time showing off and being enjoyed by his host and fellow guests, and when the meal is followed by dancing he disports himself with gusto, and is about to depart euphoric and triumphant when he suddenly realises that he's been a bit amiss in not asking his host's daughter to dance with him. In fact, he hasn't exchanged a word with her as they were sitting at opposite ends of the table during dinner. He finds her in a small room, seated at a table and attended by her companion and other ladies, and with great charm presents himself and asks her

to dance with him. Her response is a hysterical fit –
mad laughter, wails, screams etc. – and she has to
be taken away – half dragged and half carried out –
and he sees that she is paralysed from the waist
down.

Appalled by his monstrous gaffe, Anton spends
hours in an agony of shame and self-recrimination.
The following day he sends her flowers and she
invites him back to the house. He and the girl –
though she's emotionally somewhat turbulent, she
has intelligence and charm – develop a rapport. The
father, a Jew who was once a moneylender and
financial opportunist, has been devastated by first
the untimely death of his wife and then the illness
of his daughter. He welcomes Anton into the household and encourages him to become a regular visi-
tor, looking on hopefully as his daughter falls in
love. And so it unfolds from there, the story of a
young man betrayed by his own unwanted
impulses, his own timid decency. Zweig tells it with
extraordinary concentration, he follows every
bounce-bounce of feeling, from Anton's increasingly desperate attempts at disentanglement back
to guilt-ridden and resentful submission. It's
entirely Anton's story. We only know the girl from
his point of view, though there are two other characters with whom he has dealings, the father, whose

determination to fulfil his daughter's emotional needs is both moving and repellent, and a doctor who is half secular saint, half gluttonous parasite. They're both sympathetically done, but with an odd, sometimes comic, sometimes sinister edge. But really it's the way that the novel single-mindedly, almost obsessively, illustrates and analyses the destructive power of a single emotion that makes it unique, at least in my experience. I've only the last twenty or so pages to go, catastrophe looms for Anton, the girl and her father – I long for it not to, just as I long for the novel not to end, but then all things, good and bad etc. and so forth –

So there is this at least about going home, I'll find out more about Stefan Zweig, and read other things by him – we go – when? Oh, Christ, the day after tomorrow – but no need to think about that until the day after tomorrow. Well, until tomorrow anyway – anyway not tonight, when it's clear and still, and in the moonlight through the gap between the rocks I can see two little motorboats, one of them possibly the boat I saw the other night. It's the same size and shape, and there's the same large lump in the bow. The other boat is slightly larger, more obviously a fishing boat with a small hutch, a cabin, I suppose, in the middle. I can't see anyone. Can there be a bed in the cabin? There they are, rocking and swaying gently in the water. I like them there, they look attached to each other, like brother and sister – oh, something's just splashed near the side of the smaller boat, a fishing net going in, a fish jumping –

## So How Much Should We Tip Our Doctors?

We've just come back from our last swim of the holiday, of the year. Who knows when we'll have another? It wasn't a great swim, the wind is quite biting, the skies grey, rather like our first day here, so perhaps there's rain in the offing, and the sea is beginning to turn cold. Still, there were quite a lot of people on the beach, and quite a few in the sea, there must have been a batch of arrivals last night – it's the cheap end of the season, with special deals and so forth. There were young couples, some of them honeymooners, and young parents with babies, but no children over about five, no schoolchildren. There was also a fresh batch of older people, most of whom had the air of regulars, a 'yes, here we are again, good to be back' air. The only people we've seen before were the Marge Simpson twins, huddled under coats and towels, lying in the same postures as on the morning we first saw them, on their sides, smoking into each other's faces, with the dachsund settled into the curve of the stomach of one of them. Our bags are packed and have gone off. In two hours or so a taxi will come and take us to Heraklion and the airport. Victoria is in our room, packing the on-flight bags, and I'm sitting with my back against the chapel wall for the last time, writing this. I'm dreading going home but more immediately I'm dreading leaving here. For one thing there's the tipping. I've put wodges of euros in one of my trouser pockets for the restaurant people, and another wodge for the café people, and more in my top shirt pocket – I'm not at this moment wearing the trousers and shirt, they're hanging in the wardrobe in our rooms – in the shirt pocket are euros for the taxi and, oh yes, in the back pocket of my trousers I've put surplus euros in case we bump into someone that we've forgotten about. The chambermaids and the waiter who brings us our breakfast we've already tipped. We gave them theirs in envelopes, which they didn't open in front of us, so we don't know whether they're pleased or indignant – we generally overtip, knowing that if you ever get it right – give in Italy what the Italians give, in Greece what the Greeks give and so on – you're probably undertipping, as the standards for foreigners are higher, unless you're German, according to a recent article on the subject in one of the papers, when they're lower, or non-existent. Now I can tell myself that I've really got it sorted out – how could I not have, with so many contingency pockets full of euros? There's nothing else really to worry about. We've ordered the taxi for far earlier than necessary, so if it threatens to be late we'll be able to order another one and still be in good time. The airport business is always a dread – although in fact when we arrived here we got through customs and immigration in no time, the airport was completely empty except for the passengers from our plane and it gave the impression of being underused, a lonely place. The flight itself, of course, is not in our hands, so there's no point in planning for it – a drunken pilot, a defective engine, a suicide bomber, a flick of Zeus's finger – all those are the responsibility of Miracle Airlines, who have a policy of losing your bags, I hope in a kind of pact with Zeus and the rest not to lose your life –

My real dread isn't going home but being home. There will be all the compensations, the dogs George and Toto, the cats Errol and Tom, my study where I can play music again – ten days is a long time without decent music – and seeing friends, above all. I hope I won't be so embarrassed now that I've had time to get used to having cancer and they've had time to get used to my having it. My embarrassment is really a probably unjustified anticipation of their embarrassment, and this anticipation comes from shame. I know I've gone into this before, probably lots of times, but it perplexes me, this shame. I don't really believe that because I'm a smoker the cancer is self-induced. I have more than a hunch that I'd feel shame if the cancer were of the pancreas, like Alan's – there are surely no vices that result in cancer of the pancreas – although some arsehole of a government doctor will doubtless claim there is, that pancreatic cancer is caused by being famous, or not being famous when you want to be, or by being famous when you don't want to be. Or from drinking too much tea with lemon in it, or from bacon, of course – over the years many illnesses have been brought back to bacon. There's something about bacon that offends the medical profession at government level, but you have to remember that any doctor who is any good as a doctor wouldn't be working for the government, he would be doing something useful. Doctors with no sense of vocation and possessed of political skills are very dangerous, I think – look at their opposition to Chadwick and his belief in drains, sewers and hygiene in the middle of the nineteenth century, their opposition to the use of anaesthetic for operations at the start of the Crimean War, their refusal to admit that cholera was carried by contaminated water, and so forth, so forth. Oh oh! Here comes the hotel manager! He's coming down from the hotel –

## Whither Ernesto?

– he's walking along the path towards me with his trousers hitched up to his chest and his odd, disjointed but speedy gait, he's carrying a briefcase – he's seen me, for a second he slowed down, then quickened his step, does he think he can go so fast that he can get past me in a kind of blur?

No, he stopped, came to a full stop right in front of me, the briefcase swinging. He gave me his fullest smile. 'Now you go today, yes?'

'It is sad for us. For me.'

'Thank you. For us, too. Have you had a nice holiday?'

'Very nice, thank you.'

'Good. I am very happy.'

He moved off, duty done and courtesies observed, and I was about to return to my pad and report the conversation and describe again the unlikely rosiness of his complexion and the shininess of his black hair pasted flat on his scalp, when he stopped, came back and asked me whether I had arranged our taxi for the airport.

I said that I had, or rather that reception had.

'If I think of anything I can do to you, I phone you in your room, of course,' he said.

I didn't quite laugh at the thought of the various things he might think he could do to me. 'That's very kind of you, really very kind, Ernesto.'

He stopped smiling, as if there was something in my expression he didn't like, his black eyeballs had a glint in them, and he walked off abruptly, down the steps to the beach. I went to the rail to watch him. He looked anomalous, hurrying along the beach in his heavy trousers and shiny shoes and shiny hair with his shiny briefcase, passing guests in trunks and bikinis coming wet from the sea or towelling themselves. I wondered who he was going to see, why he needed his briefcase. One of the Simpson twins spotted him, sat up and called him over. The other twin sat up. From where I stood they both seemed to be talking to him at the same time, gesturing ill-temperedly with their cigarettes, evidently making a complaint. When they'd finished he spoke briefly, then made a loving reach for the dachsund, which the twin pulled away and hugged protectively to her chest. He made a little bow, then he was on his way, right to the steps at the other side. He climbed them rapidly, was gone from my sight briefly, then emerged on the path to the hotel and headed back up to it. In other words he'd made a brisk, businesslike circuit for no apparent reason. It was mysterious, what was he up to? I wondered, what was in his briefcase? but then there was something about Ernesto that never made sense, his motives were always obscure, his behaviour –

Ernesto – oh, Christ! Did I call him that? Yes, here it is, I've actually written it down. It can't be his name, Ernesto's an Italian name, surely – I'll look back and see if –

Nikos. His name is Nikos. What on earth made me call him Ernesto? It must be his personality, his hair and briefcase, his trousers – *The Importance of Being Ernesto*. Better not think of the things he'd like to do to me. Better instead to sit back in this sheltered spot and wait for Victoria to come down, I always love seeing her come along the path, her hat aslant, her straight, graceful walk, and she has a couple of very fetching wrap-arounds to cover her swimsuit – oh, but she'll be in her London clothes, and she'll tell me that it's time for me to change into mine. Socks and shoes instead of espadrilles, underpants and trousers instead of swimming trunks, a long-sleeved shirt – if only we could spend another week or two, or some months, or years, or for ever, being here, being as we've been over the last ten days – but the hotel closes at the end of the month,

all the hotels in this part of Crete close, and we have
a christening and a scan to go home to, a sort of life
to get on with.

## Privileged Treatment

Yes, yes, well we're back. We got home before midnight, and spent yesterday recovering from the
flight, though actually the flight itself wasn't too bad.
Cramped, of course, business class and cramped, but
you expect that from MA, that sort of almost criminal – no, completely criminal, in my view – swindling, but it was in fact such a relief to be on the
plane, and in the air, because the airport, Crete airport at Heraklion, which had seemed so desolately
empty when we arrived that I felt quite sorry for it
and the people who worked in it, was chaos. There
was a queue that came out on to the street and along
the pavement and out of sight. It wasn't a thin and
orderly queue, people standing in a single or double
line, it was a swollen and turbulent queue, people
jostling each other, shouting, in a panic. We wondered what flight this was, or rather the nationality
of the airline as there were far too many people for
it to be for just one flight. Inside the noise was
extraordinary – all those people trying to go through

passport control and customs, for which there was only one gate. We looked up at the flight board to see if our flight was on time and where it went from, and saw that there were seven flights leaving in the next half an hour. So the queue was seven flights' worth, with just one gate to let them through. We checked in fairly quickly. A briskly efficient girl told us that we should now go through passport control, although we had an hour and a quarter to wait – Victoria pointed this out to the girl, who said, 'Yes, yes, but it's better to go through now, it will get worse perhaps.' It was obviously hopeless. The queue was not only enormous, it seemed never to move. That was the worst thing, one didn't seem to see people actually getting through, they were wedged against the barrier, shouting, waving their tickets, children were crying, and behind them thousands more – as I've said, right through the airport and out on to the street – it was like an evacuation, with the enemy at the gates and the last planes about to take off. We sat down on a bench for a while, to rest from the shock, really, it was so unexpected, one really had hoped that this sort of thing was confined to Heathrow.

I spotted a man with a label on his shirt lapel and a walkie-talkie, into which he was talking without much urgency, quite serenely, in fact, as if he were making a call to his wife about domestic matters – but he'd do that on a mobile, surely, I thought, not on a walkie-talkie so he must be an airport official. I went over to him and waited, trying not to look too importunate. I also tried to read the writing on his label, but it was in Greek. He made a soothing gesture, to let me know that he knew I was there, went on with his conversation for a minute, then put his walkie-talkie into his belt, and gave me a charming and attentive smile. He was very good-looking in a relaxed, casual and good-humoured sort of way, a bit like Al Pacino but a foot or two taller, normal-sized in other words. 'How can I help, sir?' His English was good. I wondered why he used it before I spoke, do I look English? English-speaking? Or is the assumption that all foreigners speak English these days, and whatever I was, I couldn't be mistaken for a Cretan – too dishevelled, for one thing. And my hair. 'Well,' I said, 'I was wondering what the matter is. The queue – all the people.' I gestured towards them. 'They are going through passport control.' 'Yes, but why is it like this? Is it always like this?' 'It is often like this,' he said. 'For one reason or another. This evening, it is because there is only one police officer looking at the passports.' 'Won't a lot of them miss their planes?' He thought about it. 'Sometimes it happens. Sometimes yes.' I tried to find a tactful way of asking what his official position was – he was so friendly and easy – 'What do you do,' I asked, cleverly I thought, 'if people get left behind?' 'What do I do?' he said with a shrug of his shoulders and his friendly smile. 'I do nothing. What can I do? This is Greece.' He took his walkie-talkie out of his pocket and listened, then said something in a Scandinavian language, fluently and slightly flirtatiously – but then he was obviously by nature flirtatious.

I went back to Victoria and said that all I'd gathered was that this shambles was quite usual, that sometimes people missed their planes, but I couldn't vouch for the source of this information, as I had no idea who he was or what he did, or even his nationality. 'Are you all right?' she said. 'Yes,' I said, but I wasn't, my legs were dissolving under me, and I felt as if I was going to fall down. 'Here,' she said, 'sit down.' She gave me her seat, as someone had taken mine, a pleasantly impassive Oriental girl. I slumped there, looking at the queue that hadn't changed, the same people still seemed to be at the front of it, still holding up their tickets and clamouring, and once again it had got fatter, now almost double the size it had been when we arrived – Well, there was one thing I knew for certain, I couldn't join it, I suspected I couldn't stand by myself for long, I could hardly keep my head up.

Victoria brought me a chocolate bar. I tore its wrapping off and guzzled it down with uninhibited greed, behaving as I behave every night when alone, a disgusting spectacle. I didn't look up to see whether I was being observed and when I finished I demanded another one. 'Sorry, darling, need another one,' is what I think I said. She'd bought three, and I ate them all, the third one rather more decorously, and though I felt sick when I'd finished, and had a headache, I felt stronger. I could stand up and walk a few paces, not exactly steadily, but in a steady direction at least. I sat down again and Victoria went off to get some water. She also suggested she get me a wheelchair – there was a time, before my hip replacement, when I'd had to go through airports in a wheelchair, and I'd hated it, believing it was more honourable to totter along with a stick and the support of my wife – it was one of the many pleasures of being able to walk properly again that I could deal with airports like a normal passenger – so I said no, I can manage, I'll be all right – though really I knew this was nonsense – but I also thought that, well, we could always spend the night in Heraklion, leave tomorrow.

Victoria brought the water. She also brought a pretty young woman, blonde, in an MA uniform, with a harsh, bossy voice, who told me to wait where I was, went off for a few minutes and returned leading a wheelchair procession – young people with casts on their legs and necks, an obese man in his fifties with curly grey hair who was wearing red swimming trunks and a soiled white T-shirt with an image of a bare-breasted girl riding a motorbike stamped on it, and several elderly and frail-looking men and women, clasping sticks. Behind each wheelchair was a pusher, presumably a partner, though some looked ill-assorted – in the case of one of the frail old men there was a seemingly much frailer old woman pushing him, and the obese man with the T-shirt was being pushed by a campy young fellow in purple trousers and a yellow shirt who kept fluting, 'Hold on there, Rodge, we'll be on in a jiff!' while Rodge chortled and mumbled to himself, possibly he was drunk or brain-damaged. Well, this lot was my cortège, so to speak. I walked at the head of it, Victoria at one side and at the other, just in front of me, the blonde MA girl, who shouted instructions in her hoarse, abrasive voice, in both English and Greek, in English 'Out of the way please, out of the way,' and in Greek presumably much the same. The people at the head of the queue surged towards us mutinously and then fell away when they saw what we were, it was a sort of miracle, really, as if I were leading a group of ill and maimed to Lourdes, so much respect, amounting to reverence, did this hitherto desperate and panic-stricken mob give us, watching us with sorrowful eyes as we passed through them. I don't know what they made of me, looking tanned and healthy, even if I was drooping a little. Perhaps they assumed I was there in a medical capacity.

We went straight through passport control, where two officers, not just one, were studying every passport with academic thoroughness as we approached, but hardly glanced at ours, then security and customs – and we were on the other side, where we could settle down and wait calmly for our call. It came punctually. We left on time. I fell asleep at once, before we were in the air – the first time in my life I've slept through an entire flight – and was scarcely awake during the drive from Gatwick.

When we got home I said hello to all the animals, and went to bed, where I stayed for much of yesterday. Now I'm up and about. Tomorrow is Saturday, the christening. I would think that Crete was a dream, if I didn't remember the time at the airport so vividly. And then there's the tan, visible on my arms below my rolled-up shirt sleeves and on the backs of my hands, as I sit writing this –

# London

# Eli Takes Centre Stage

The christening was at Farm Street Church, a famous and fashionable Catholic church in Mayfair, which I hadn't been to before. It looked very swanky at three o'clock this afternoon, bathed in sunlight with little groups of well-dressed people, many of the ladies in hats and one or two of the gents in morning suits – relaxed and elegant, there was a touch of Ascot about it, not that I've been to Ascot. At the bottom of the street, waiting in the wings, so to speak, were Toby, his wife, Annie-Lou, and in Annie-Lou's arms their baby son, Eli. Annie-Lou looked sensational in a sensationally short skirt and a very elegant top which I didn't really notice as I couldn't take my eyes off her legs, they were so long and shapely. Toby was wearing a natty suit and a waistcoat, I think – perhaps it was a morning suit. We stood outside the church on the pavement watching them come towards us. I honestly don't think I've seen such a beautiful couple, a beautiful trio, really, because Eli, as yet only a scrap at five months, has a beautifully shaped head off which the sun seemed to strike so that it glittered. We did some kissing and so forth and then went inside. Dame Maggie Smith, the fortunate grandmother to Eli, emerged from behind a pillar to say hello, and then we – Victoria and I – were led to our pew, the godparents' pew, right at the front on the left facing the altar, on the other side of the aisle from the parents and Eli. There was another godparent, a smiling young woman, a cousin – well, I think cousin – of Annie-Lou already ensconced. She seemed pleased to see us, and we were certainly pleased to see her. None of us had acted as Catholic godparents before,* none of us being Catholic, but at least we could give each other moral support – in fact I always look to Victoria in this sort of situation, believing that she has an innate understanding of the ceremonies of life, even though, like me, it's a long time since she's been in a church – we used to go every Christmas to our local, at the top of our street, but gave up when one year at the end of the service the vicar asked us to handshake and cuddle fellow members of the congregation, most of whom I didn't like the look of, and one of whom, a distraught, middle-aged woman, threw herself into people's arms, tears of love and joy running down her cheeks – 'Bless you, bless you,' she cried, as she bounced from bosom to bosom – so we felt slightly ill at ease being back in a church again,

* Victoria has many other godchildren and I have one, Simon Hammerstein, of many years' standing.

even one where you could expect calm and dignified behaviour. In fact the atmosphere, though calm
and dignified, was also cheerful and relaxed, with
people meeting up and chatting in the aisle, and children skirmishing at the front and sides, and popping
out from behind the pews. Under the circumstances
it was quite difficult, even for inexperienced and
unrehearsed godparents, to feel nervous and in fact
all that really worried me was that I might have to
hold Eli, and have a sudden weak spell and drop
him on the stone floor, head first – It would be difficult to live that down, a godfather who killed his
godchild at the christening. I decided, if by any
chance Eli was passed to me, I'd pass him straight
on to Victoria, whatever the convention. The vicar
came in, no, presumably not the vicar, the priest,
whatever – and moved about, shaking hands and
being sociable, then went to the front and, in an easy,
conversational manner, began the service – service, I
suppose that's the right word for it. The priest – let's
call him that – the priest was astonishingly like the
English film actor of many years ago, Wilfrid Hyde-
White, noted for his hooded eyes and his sleazy
charm. But the priest's eyes were only slightly
hooded and his charm wasn't in the slightest sleazy,
the resemblance was more in the appearance, same
height, same hair, same sort of age that Wilfrid

Hyde-White always appeared to be – about sixty, even when young – and same timbre of voice. He was beguiling, especially in his concentration on five-month-old Eli. He addressed everything important directly to him and not to the congregation, and Eli, now in his beautiful mother's arm, returned the compliment by fixing his baby gaze on him with rapt and devoted concentration – it was both funny and moving, the loveliest sight I've ever seen in a church, the elderly man and the wide-eyed baby in earnest consultation, the elderly man speaking a language that the rest of us recognised and understood, and yet seemed to contain within it another and private language recognised and understood by the baby –

The godparents' turn came about halfway through. We had first of all to give a number of solemn undertakings. I can't say I felt easy about any of them, even the basic ones of resisting the temptations of the devil, and making false promises. I suspect that there are one or two temptations I would be quite pleased to have the devil offer me at the moment, and I really don't see how you can manage a career as a playwright without making a false promise now and then, after all so many are made to you – by actors, directors, producers, who insist that one day, absolutely certainly one day, they'll do this or that play of yours – equally, one day, I say, I'll write a play you'll want to do, I know I will. So really I felt a bit odd about not making false promises, suspecting that I'd actually made one in undertaking not to. But the most difficult bit was when we, the two god-mothers and the one godfather, were asked whether we were prepared to make sure that Eli was brought up in the Catholic faith. There wasn't a distinct sound from any of us, just an ambiguous mumble, and then the priest, probably knowing the situation, passed fluently on. Eli loved the actual baptism, which was – cunningly – with warm water. He gurgled with pleasure and it was a joy when it was my turn to dab his forehead and have him gurgle at me. And that was it, really, my godfatherly duty had been to speak lies before God and then to stand at the font and lie again in dumbshow by assisting in a religious cere-mony that had, for me, no spiritual significance. And yet very little in these last few years has given me so much pleasure and made me so proud, and Victoria, I know, feels the same, and though we can't do any-thing for the Catholic side of Eli's life, we've made a start on the many other sides by presenting him with specially bound copies of the whole of Shakespeare, with his initials on the spine.

Afterwards we went to Annie-Lou's parents' place for drinks and such. I began to feel tired, had an attack of weakness and had to sit down. Annie-Lou introduced Victoria to a friend of her parents, a very lively and intelligent woman who knew a great deal about the treatment of cancer in America, and particularly of a man in California, a specialist in a new form of chemotherapy. Someone else had told us about this man and had spoken as highly of him as did this woman, whose husband had been treated by him. Victoria told me afterwards, because I wasn't able to concentrate properly, that she said that he was remarkable. Unlike so many doctors he had a wide range of interests, including an interest in his patients, what they did, what they thought about, what they read, their favourite music, that sort of interest. Furthermore he was a genius and a miracle worker. Her husband, who'd gone to California to be treated by him, had gone to him far too late and refused a final course of chemo because he needed to get home to England to die, but right to the end had shared his wife's enthusiasm for the man in California.

## Servitude

We left and came home and I went to bed, but couldn't sleep. I got up and here I am, the established godfather of Eli, writing this – and now there is something making a disturbance at my door, it's a soft noise, difficult to describe, but it's as if someone were beating a small cushion against it, causing it to tremble slightly. I know perfectly well who it is. It's Errol, our big black bushy cat who came out of nowhere one day, intruded himself through the dog flap and set up as a lodger. He made an immediate and close friendship with our half-westie bitch, George, but was hostile to Tom, our elderly black and white female cat, treating her as if she were an undesirable squatter and sitting bulkily in front of the dog flap whenever she went out to stop her coming in again.

On the other hand, when we introduced a second dog, a terrier called Toto, into the household Errol welcomed her and made a fuss of her, eating as affectionately from her bowl as from George's, sleeping sometimes between her paws, at other times between George's, a dog's cat, you might say, although he's good with humans too. Now, some six years later, he and Tom get on reasonably well. He's prepared to defer, I think, to Tom's great age – she's twenty-one. They touch noses when they meet in the hall, and lie side by side on the warm spot on the floor outside the kitchen and when in a minute or two I go to the door which Errol is butting with his head, I will find Tom sitting beside him, waiting. When I open the door Tom will screech at me ill-temperedly, then turn and follow Errol downstairs to the kitchen, occasionally looking over her shoulder to make sure I'm following, and, if I'm slow or too far behind, give another screech. I will go to the larder and take out a packet of jellied meat for Errol, and hoist up a large sack of nodules for Tom and put it on the table. Tom's and Errol's bowls are on the counter of the dresser. I will fill Errol's bowl with the jellied meat and then – in spite of the fact that he can climb to the counter by way of a chair placed there for that very purpose, and in spite of the fact that he can scale and leap like a mountain goat when food is his quest – I will have to bend down and pick him up and place him in front of his bowl. Then I will have to pick up Tom, who is also perfectly capable of reaching the counter on her own, and put her in front of her bowl, which she refuses to touch, even if it's half full or completely full of nodules, until I have put, or pretended to put, more nodules in it. Then I can leave them to themselves and go back to my study. I have no idea why they both insist on being picked up. I suspect it's something to do with dominance, their need to keep me in my place as both provider and servant. Sometimes I don't mind, in fact the ritual is reassuring, but these days I find Errol a real weight, bending down and lifting him has made me feel faint once or twice, and I resent it. Tom is an easy lift, her body is light with age and she lies almost weightless in my hand, but – well, I've caught myself looking at her when she creaks as if broken-backed up the stairs, or wakes from one of her long sleeps and stumbles about before finding her balance – 'Yes, but for all that –' and I've said it aloud to her, quite bitterly, 'for all that, you'll be here, creaking about, when I'm gone.'*

## A Living Bower? Oh, for God's Sake!

I had the scan this afternoon. Really it was simple and efficient, only a five-minute wait and then I was under the machine, a voice calling out from a protected booth when to breathe and when to hold my breath, and I was finished and joining Victoria at a table outside the pub. The bad part of it is that Dr Rootle is away – it's half-term, apparently, so he might be on a holiday with the wife and kids, or he might be at a conference in Beijing, for example – all I know is that it's a week and a day until we see him, and find out the results of the scan – whether I am to have more radiotherapy, or am promoted to chemotherapy, or go on as I'm going on at the moment.

Before we left the pub we discussed whether to give me a birthday party. We'd given them now and

* She won't. She died shortly after I wrote that passage.

then over the years, and usually I'd enjoyed them enormously when they were over, thinking that they would be markers in my memory – not so much little tombstones on the way to the final, big tombstone, but milestones on a winding, complex journey of ever-extending length, or living bowers of remembrance or some such – and in fact when I do look back on them I have a general sense of muzzy, unfocused pleasure for most of them, with sharp, painful details sticking out from some of them – there was one in my fifties, for instance, when a young fan of a guest, more stalker than fan, happened to be in the club where the party was being given, and invaded it for a while. He was drunk and full of pot, the personification of malice, envy and worship all mixed up – the worship unsatisfied as the guest who was the object of it, a famous actor, sent him on his way with gentle authority. He responded with mutinous obedience in that he took his humble leave of the famous actor but then went lurching from table to table delivering his opinion of all the people in the room he recognised, and also of those he didn't recognise but whose appearance stimulated his venom. I knew him quite well, and finally got him outside on the pavement. I smoked cigarettes while he smoked joints, and we made vile, conspiratorial conversation until I lured him into a taxi and sent him into the night. He only took up half an hour of a party that began at nine and ended in the early hours of the morning. I doubt if anyone else would remember him, or took much notice of him at the time – a stoned and hostile young man who intruded briefly at your table was not a significant event unless you were the host – but, as I've said, he's all I remember with any distinctness, and as for the rest of the evening, all I can say is that I believe it went well enough but I can't be sure.

The fact is that a party given on my behalf makes me nervous, and then as the date grows closer I actively dread it – more even than I dread a first night – but then a first night is a shared responsibility, you, the director, the actors and the producers are all in it together, at least until the reviews come out to separate you – frequently and specifically me, the playwright, with such sentences as, 'Not even Oliver Gilboy playing three parts can save a play that should be booed, hooted and raspberried off the stage.' But from then on you can conceal yourself, stay indoors for a year or two or go to restaurants where people won't have read the reviews because they never read the reviews of anything and may not be able to read anyway, as opposed to your usual restaurants, where there will be people who will have read the reviews several times but who will pretend not to have, and will call out, 'Simon, how did it go, what were the reviews like? Madge was telling me about the ones in the *Guardian* and *The Times* and the *Telegraph*, but I can't remember what she said they said –' and if you claim – as has been true in recent years – that you don't read them, they will reply, 'Good for you, because I gather from what Madge said that they weren't worth reading.' But my point is that even the anticipation of a first night and the next day's reviews is better than the anticipation of a party, a birthday party above all, and what – according to Dr Rootle – would be a birthday party on my last birthday. I feared I might find myself looking around at all the familiar, beloved (well, many of them) faces, thinking sombre thoughts and possibly bursting into tears when my health was proposed – that sort of thing. This would make it memorable, though not to me, of course, as I wouldn't, again given Dr Rootle's estimate, be around long enough to make it a memory. But perhaps it's a pleasing thought that my guests would remember it, making the doleful but moving connection – 'Just fancy, his last birthday was his last ever and he knew, of course! How very, very, very moving!' – we went over the pros and cons for a while, and before we left I think we settled it that we'd either have a party or we wouldn't, we'd talk about it again later, or perhaps we wouldn't –

# A Disaster Remembered

Harold came out of hospital a couple of days ago but is still, Antonia said, very weak, couldn't go out, but would welcome a visit, she thought. I phoned him and though he sounded thin and far away, he said he'd like it if I looked in. He was in his usual armchair, with a fire blazing in the grate, its flames orange and blue. I gave him a book I'd brought for him, then sat in the armchair opposite, on the other side of the fire. He looked into the book, Keith Miller's autobiography, written over fifty years ago, which I bought second-hand over forty years ago and is long out of print. I thought Harold would like and be touched by the photographs, the sort you don't see any more, grey and white and one-dimensional, the men with Brylcreemed hair and smiling, shiny faces, and the clothes, of course – the cricketers either in long-sleeved white shirts and creased white flannels belted tightly at the waist, or in drab grey suits with fedoras and trilbies. The prose is cheerful and kindly, lots of anecdotes but no gossip, nothing revealed but the spirit of the age and the modest decency of the writer, who was, in fact, also a gambler and a womaniser, one of Princess Margaret's lovers and a bit of a home-wrecker and so forth, as well as a war hero – an incomparable man, really.

Harold dipped into a few places, smiled and grunted, put the book down and we looked at each other. So here we were, two elderly and ailing men who'd known each other for half our lifetimes. We talked bitterly about the things that were most on our minds – sickness, hospitals, colonoscopies, catheters, the sheer helplessness and humiliation of it all. His voice got stronger the longer we talked, and we both got more cheerful, the absurdity of it, that such things could be happening to us, who in so many important respects hadn't yet reached our maturity, we still had miles to go before we slept, miles to go.

After we'd been at it for about an hour or so I thought he must be getting tired. I was feeling a little tired myself and was on the point of getting up when he reached for the book. 'Thanks for this,' he said, opened it, looked closely at one of the photographs, and remarked that there was going to be the annual meeting of his cricket club, the Gaieties, in a few days' time, he wouldn't be able to go himself, he said, wouldn't be up to it, but they'd asked him if he'd do a little speech on video, and he'd decided that this was what he was going to tell them –

That in one of his first matches as captain the opposing side's best batsman was in, and going ominously well until he skied a catch, very high, with Harold directly under it. He mimed himself gazing anxiously upwards, then jerking from side to side to get into the right position, then cupping his hands, then watching the ball as it fell through his hands and dropped at his feet. The next ball the batsman repeated the shot, the ball went up, came down through Harold's hands to land once again at his feet. The batsman went on to make a hundred. It came to the Gaieties' turn to bat. Their best batsman was going promisingly well, with a big score and possibly victory in sight, when a wicket fell and Harold came out to join him. In no time Harold had run him out. A few balls later Harold was bowled neck and crop. The Gaieties lost by an enormous margin, entirely because of Harold's versatile performance.

It was as if we were suddenly many years ago, back having a boozy lunch in our favourite restaurant, L'Epicure, Romilly Street, a week before rehearsals. He finished with a broken cry of despair, as if he could still see the ball at his feet, hear the stumps rattle behind him, and we both laughed and laughed until we both coughed and coughed, laughed and coughed –

# Why I Bought So Much Cheese

Walking home from Harold's down Holland Park Avenue, I felt quite sprightly, yes, really quite sprightly. I saw Annabelle outside Tesco's, tootling her recorder, her dog at her feet. Annabelle is a local beggar, no, one of the two local beggars. They're partners, I think, although in what sense of the word isn't really clear. I know she has grandchildren but not whether he's the grandfather. They seem to have a fairly intense and complicated relationship, working within fifty or so yards of each other, he sitting on the pavement, with competent if insipid watercolours of beaches and harbours, meadows and woodlands, she with her recorder and dog. They're often in earnest, whispering confabulation together, and just as often having hateful exchanges, standing not facing each other but sideways on, speaking out of the sides of their mouths, and then one or the other flounces off. Though to me they're Annabelle and Hyacinth, I have no idea what their real names are – I forget why I called her Annabelle, just from a desire to name her, I suppose. I called him Hyacinth after the Henry James character Hyacinth Robinson in *The Princess Casamassima* for reasons now obscure to me as I no longer remember the novel. I could see that she'd seen me. Her eyes were now fixed on me. She was expecting me to come to her with a handful of cigarettes or some money.

For once I wasn't in the mood for Annabelle. She can have a lowering effect on my spirits, particularly in the soft evening sunshine, and though she never asks for anything, she is somehow importunate, she aims her recorder at you, and her eyes search out yours. Hyacinth is easier, as he's down on the pavement, below one's eye level, and one can pretend he's not there. If he croaks out a greeting one can lift one's hand in vague but benevolent salute as one scoots past. In fact, I didn't spot him in the vicinity this evening. There was just Annabelle, expectant. So I thought, oh well, give her something and get it over with, and then realised that as I no longer carry cigarettes in my pocket, and as I had no money apart from a twenty-pound note, I had nothing to give her, so without consciously planning to I swung into Tesco's. There was nothing I wanted in Tesco's, there is never anything I want in Tesco's. If occasionally they introduce a line that actually appeals to me they withdraw it the moment they know I've begun buying it. So I didn't go right into the shop, I stood to the side of the door, out of her sight, and waited for her to trap someone

227

else and then I'd slip out, was my vague plan.

Actually she's quite a popular figure, Annabelle. People know her and stop to exchange a few words, give her a coin, pass on, but this evening, perhaps because it was so lovely, people felt as I did and gave her a miss. One couple even crossed the road to avoid her, because I saw them cross back again at the next traffic lights. The security chap by the door began giving me quick, appraising glances. Of course these days, an elderly man hanging about on his own in a busy shop must be up to no good, almost certainly about to practise some senile form of sexual deviance. I had the feeling that he was going to come over and question me at any moment, so I decided to get on with it, take my chances with Annabelle. I'd make a brisk enquiry after her health and be on my way as she was answering me. I went out, she moved a step or so towards me, lowering the recorder and with one hand extended – she's quite pretty, Annabelle, have I said that? young-looking for a grandmother, at least her face is. She keeps it blank when just standing waiting and when receiving money even from people she knows well, just saying in a lifeless mutter, 'Thank you very much, I reelly appreciate it,' but if she's engaged in a proper conversation her face becomes animated, her previously dull, almost lifeless eyes glint with humour, sometimes sly and malicious humour, and she becomes, well, not exactly attractive but –

Well, actually it's impossible to talk about her body as she's made it bulky and shapeless by the dark bits and pieces in which she clothes herself, they don't look like garments, but like large pieces of cloth ripped from larger pieces of cloth. She wears them in layers, wrapped around the top part of herself and hanging from her waist, and one or sometimes two wrapped around her head and tied under her chin.

Anyway, there she was, coming towards me, with her hand extended, not in an actual begging position. I've never heard either Annabelle or Hyacinth ask for anything except the time – a tactic for stopping people, luring them into conversation, a situation from which donations may flow – but even so there was the sense of an appeal in the way she was holding out her hand, an emotional appeal, for help and comfort in distress, perhaps, though the truth is I couldn't bear to look at it properly, her hands are the worst thing about her, visibly, anyway – they're filthy, as are the fingernails, broken and jagged and dark yellow from nicotine, the nicotine stain seems to go right into the palm of the hand, a hand you hope you will never, ever, have to touch, and the sight of which made it easier for me to hustle around her with, 'Evening, how are you? OK are you, eh?' and then I was away, smoothly enough.

I sensed rather than heard her pattering up behind me, and then she was muttering in my ear – 'He's dead. He's dead, you see, Simon.' Well, of course, I had to stop, turn around and face her. 'He's dead,' she said again, with exactly the blank expression and in exactly the toneless voice that she uses when she says, 'Thank you very much, I reelly appreciate it.' Her hand was still held out, and it struck me that she was asking me to take it, clasp it. 'Who's dead?' 'My friend,' she said. 'What, Hyacinth!' I exclaimed. 'Good God!' Her blank expression went blanker, from bewilderment. 'Who?' 'Oh, I mean your friend – um?' 'Yes,' she said. She named him. I can't remember what name, I was confused with embarrassment, really, at having forgotten that I'd never told Hyacinth and Annabelle what their names were. 'I'm dreadfully sorry,' I said. 'So very sorry, how exactly did he –?' She said his liver had given out, he'd collapsed, been rushed to St Mary's, Paddington, and died there three days ago. 'We been friends thirteen years,' she added, or was it seventeen, anyway it was an odd number, not a rounded one, and she made it sound very specific, as if it were important. Thirteen as opposed to fourteen or twelve, or seventeen as opposed to sixteen or eighteen. So for thirteen or possibly seventeen years they'd been friends. Her cupped hand, which had the appeal of a soiled lavatory bowl, was still cupped and wagging itself at me. 'Well, I'm so sorry,' I said again, thinking, Oh, Christ, I'll have to do something! 'Look,' I said, 'look, I'll see you, eh?' and stepped away from her, and walked down Holland Park Avenue wondering whether I should give her the twenty, and then thinking that no, I shouldn't, because a) it might seem that I was trying to pay her off for her grief and b) I didn't want to, it was too much.

I went into Jeroboams and looked at the cheeses, my intention being, not to buy her cheese for consolation but to buy myself a cheese and give her a few quid from the change – it's a long time since I've bought cheese, and I've never known much about them, so I selected rather randomly, pointing to a French goat's cheese because it looked like one I used to eat in Clermont-Ferrand, where I taught English to trainee chefs and waiters in 1956, and then a Cheddar, then a blue and white one, then a round Dutch one. I got into the swing of it, overcoming my usual indecisiveness by pointing at any cheese that caught my eye. The problem was that I had no idea, when it came to cutting them into portions, how much I wanted, as the question was put to me in terms of weight. I finished up with an enormous carrier bag of cheeses plus some luxury chocolate bars and a bag of ginger snaps, I hope they are, and as it came to just over twenty quid I had to pay with my credit card and so still had nothing for Annabelle.

She was back standing outside Tesco's, talking to an old-fashioned middle-aged man in a suit. He was fumbling in his pocket, and she was looking impassively past him, straight at me. I went a few yards down, into the newsagent, and bought a packet of cigarettes, Silk Cut, and got back a ten-pound note and under five pounds in change. I walked towards Annabelle, who pretended not to see me. She put the recorder to her lips and tootled at it unmusically. I couldn't help suspecting she was being satirical. When I got to her she put the recorder down, and I put into her hand the change, which she put into a bag at her waist, 'Thank you very much, I reely appreciate it,' she said in her receiver's voice. I handed her the packet of cigarettes and, though she didn't change her tone or vocabulary, she added my name. 'Thank you very much, Simon. I reely appreciate it, Simon,' and then, 'He was my friend for seventeen years, Simon' – though, as I've said, it might have been thirteen years, thus directly and uncomplicatedly connecting my gifts to Hyacinth's death. Well, I'd rather give her cigarettes and money than write her a letter of condolence about Hyacinth's passing, I thought, as I went on down the avenue, swinging the heavy bag of assorted cheeses. Thank God Victoria loves cheese, though I have an idea she's trying to stop eating it as she suspects it's bad for her, has, in fact, stopped buying it –

The thing about Hyacinth is that the last time I saw him, about four days ago, he was in a floral shirt and jeans, his hair tied back in a pigtail, he was foraging in a litter bin and looked appalling, scrawny and gaunt, his eyes so sunk that his face seemed to be all jaw and brow and his body was trembling and I thought the sort of thought I've been having about Tom, our ancient cat – yes, well, you've been there before, Hyacinth, at the grave's edge, but you'll be back on the pavement with your feeble watercolours eventually, and you'll outlive me, won't you? and the thought made me angry, not with him, but with who knows what, whatever is responsible for these things.

## What If, One Day, He's Not There?

There's a small bearded man in a peaked cap with a bent-forward walk, as if he's battling strong winds, who passes by Kensington Place at roughly the same time every evening – well, every evening we've been there, and as we sometimes go to Kensington Place two or three times a week and have been going there for the last ten years, it's not logically correct but perfectly reasonable to assume that he goes past our table every evening, whether we're sitting at it or not. Very often, but not always, we also see him coming back about half an hour later, walking with the same bent-forward walk, which is how I know that he's not battling the wind, unless the wind changes to the opposite direction for the specific purpose of blowing against him. He has a very peaceful if determined face, rather philosophical, and it's possible that like Immanuel Kant he takes a constitutional at the same time and follows the same route every day, although one night –

We pointed him out to friends who frequently eat with us at Kensington Place. One night the four of us went to another restaurant in the same neighbourhood, but at a considerable distance from it. When we came out and were standing on the pavement kissing goodnight and so forth, he suddenly appeared at the top of the street, bending forward as usual, and walked past us. We froze, the four of us, in astonishment, believing for the moment that his usual route must actually be any route that took him past us, wherever we happened to be. Then we wondered if he weren't a hallucination that had belonged first to Victoria and me, and now to anyone who joined us for a meal in Notting Hill, and then of course it occurred to us that it was a simple coincidence, that his was a long looping constitutional that took him past Kensington Place, then on past this restaurant and then round and back past Kensington Place –

So everything we need to understand about this man is now understood. There is no mystery or need for a supernatural explanation. He is simply a man of mechanically regular habits. I long to know what work he does, whether he's married and has children. He seems a solitary, a lifelong solitary, not a widower. I have begun to worry about him. Now when we go to Kensington Place I keep an eye out, and I get increasingly anxious until he appears. He hasn't failed me yet, but I wonder what I'll feel if one night he doesn't come. I suspect that I've attached my fate to his continuing to trudge, bent forward and resolute, along the pavement past our table –

He came tonight, thank God, his scarf flowing behind him – I don't think I've mentioned his scarf, it's grey and very long, and sometimes almost horizontal, as if to emphasise the strength of the wind he is battling against. The reason I was so relieved to see him is that tomorrow we go to Dr Rootle for the results of the scan, but not until late in the afternoon. How will I get through the hours leading up to it?

Dr Johnson said that knowing you're going to be hanged in the morning concentrates the mind wonderfully. Supposing you won't know until the morning whether you're going to be hanged in the morning? What does that do to the mind?

## A Distraction from Distraction: Tonight

Well, right now I'll keep myself distracted by writing about – by writing about – oh yes, Stefan Zweig, why not? I've spent the last week or so reading as much of him as I could get my hands on and I've looked him up on Google, where I discovered that he was an immensely popular and successful author in the 1920s and early 1930s, a worldwide bestseller, particularly loved and admired in France, in Germany and in his native Austria – and he still is in France, where you can buy translations of his short stories and novellas at railway stations and airports. He also did well in the United States, but was never quite taken up by the English – I don't know why and my source in Google offers no explanation. Now I'm English, can I offer an explanation? Well for one thing he likes to write about women, he has a feeling for their feelings – *Twenty-four Hours in the Life of a Woman*, for instance, is about a composed and attractive widow who spots a young man gambling in a casino at a fashionable resort, is struck by the intensity of his play, catches the despair in his eyes and on impulse follows him when he runs out, to find him sitting on a bench contemplating suicide. She determines to save him, spends the night with him in a turmoil of sex and sacrifice, and then gets together some money and gives it to him, after making him promise that he'll give up gambling, return to his family and pay off his debts. And then – and then – well, the end is predictable almost from the first moment that she sees him, and in spite of the urgency of the writing – even in translation Zweig is a fluently urgent and impassioned writer – one doesn't care much. The fact is that gamblers, like all addicts, are pretty boring in that their lives tend to follow one of two narratives, they either struggle heroically to give up and succeed, or they struggle less heroically and fail, there is very little room for variety in either tale, and the thing about Zweig's storytelling is that he is so earnestly insistent, sometimes almost pleading with us to feel as the woman

237

feels, care as she cares – and of course the more he insists and pleads the more we resist – and yet there's such decency and kindness in his writing, his tone of voice I mean, that one feels a touch mean-spirited – and one resents that too, a bit – one really wishes one didn't find him somewhat phoney and melodramatic – Christ, it's past dawn, there's sunlight and the birds, the bloody birds – bed, bed, must go to bed, two co-proxamol and a sleeper, no, two sleepers – no, try and make do with one.

## The Same Distraction from the Same Distraction

I've been up for an hour, two hours to go before we leave the house, if I could trust myself I wouldn't go, I'd say I feel OK, not exactly well but not really ill, let sleeping tumours lie etc., but of course I've got to find out for sure – he's bound to give me bad news, probably reduce my life expectancy, which according to his previous prediction is now down to eight months – I should think I've used up two or three of those in destructive emotions but now, this morning, I feel, apart from the fear, abnormally calm, accepting that whatever the news there is nothing I can do to change it – I can neither make it worse by smoking a couple of panicky cigarettes nor make it better by not smoking them, so now the second one is smouldering in my ashtray, I lift it to my lips sometimes as I write this, but don't draw the smoke deep in my lungs, I let it swirl in my throat and linger there before blowing it out – now where did I stop? On what? Oh yes, Zweig, my last sentence was about, oh yes, *Twenty-four Hours in the Life of a Woman* – that I didn't really believe any of it – now what other stories have I read? There's – oh yes, *Amok*, well, I didn't believe that, either, I remember that much, but what was it about? Think now. Concentrate.

Ah yes. The narrator is travelling on a steamer from Calcutta to Europe, he comes across a fellow passenger skulking about the deck at night, drinking and distraught and desperate to tell his story, which our narrator passes on to us exactly as it was told to him, in fact in direct speech, I think, only inserting himself to set the scenes of their various meetings and to describe the man's tone of voice, his glittering eye, his frantic manner – the story the man tells is this: that, yes, that eight years ago he'd been a successful young doctor with a good post in a big hospital in Leipzig, had met a beautiful woman with an imperial manner and an icy heart, for whom he had stolen money from the hospital funds. The scandal was hushed up by an uncle who found him a job in a wretched and swampy outpost of the colonies – Dutch East Indies, I think – where he festers away from drink, loneliness and boredom, nothing but animals and natives for company until one day an English woman of evident class and breeding and with a somewhat haughty manner turns up, having come all the many miles from the colonial capital. She has somehow heard of his skills and hints that she's after an abortion.

The doctor, out of a confusion of unruly feelings along with a perfectly understandable desire for revenge on coldly beautiful women, says he will help her only if she a) asks him outright for what she wants from him, i.e. an abortion, and b) gives him what she knows he wants from her, i.e. her body. She refuses and sweeps indignantly off.

He sets out to find her and when he does so (at a society ball in the colonial capital) mumbles out abject apologies for the foulness of his behaviour and begs her to let him perform the operation before it becomes dangerous, it's already nearly too late – she rejects his offer and evades his overtures until it's actually too late, then sends her Chinese servant, who has, if I remember correctly, a 'moist, dog-like but determined gaze', to bring him to a squalid backstreet hideaway, where she is lying blood-soaked and in agony from a botched abortion. He and the Chinese dog-like boy clean her up – no, no, I can't go on with this.

The truth is that even as I write the plot down every sentence strikes me as so preposterous that I can't believe that I'm remembering it accurately – but then I found it pretty preposterous when I was reading it, it's chock-a-block with the sort of coincidences that only happen in life, should never happen in fiction – what's the time?

## This Afternoon: Thank You, Stefan Zweig, Thank You

So. So. Yes, there's something I said above, to the effect that often with Zweig I don't trust the narrator – it's a peculiar thing about quite a few of the stories I've read, they're not told directly by Zweig, they're told to him by someone he meets, and then passed on to us in a first-person narrative that is therefore in inverted commas – this is true of *Amok* and also of *Beware of Pity*. It's as if Zweig needed to shift the responsibility for his imagination on to someone else – and this odd sort of evasiveness is there in his autobiography, what's it called, terrible title, hopelessly unmemorable, anyway he presents himself so completely as a representative figure of his age, born and

241

nurtured in the golden and dying days of the Austro-Hungarian Empire, with no sense at all that his Jewishness separated him from the world of Viennese culture – then came the First World War and its havoc, followed by a decade of peace that for him was a decade of growing success and international fame, and then suddenly, inexplicably, there was Hitler, and Zweig's highly acclaimed and immensely popular books made part of the bonfire, and then there were the concentration camps, which plucked from their homes his colleagues and friends and were reaching out for him too, for after all he was known to be a Jew, even if he hadn't really known it himself until then – not even his collaboration with Strauss, Hitler's favourite living composer, could save him, and anyway, when it came to it, he didn't want to be saved, not in that sense – so what was left but flight and exile?

He went to London, then to Bath, then to America, and from there to Brazil – why Brazil, when he had so many friends in New York? The edition I have ends with his suicide letter, written in Petropolis in 1942, in which he thanks the people of Brazil for welcoming him into their midst, states that he's leaving the world while still in full possession of his health and faculties because all he sees for the future of Europe, his spiritual home, is nightmare – death the only refuge. In fact he sees himself as a forerunner, others will surely follow, he will await them, although he doesn't say exactly where – although perhaps I've misremembered that bit. Anyway, it's a stately and gracious letter, more like a letter of resignation than a suicide letter, with only glancing reference to his much younger wife, and after all he took her with him – or she elected to go with him, let's rather say. They were found dead in their bed from an overdose of barbiturates, their hands clasped – is that right, about their hands, or have I added it in? Victoria's just rung from her study to say that we have to leave in half an hour, am I ready? I said yes, yes I am –

Now where – yes, well, so what's disconcerting about the book – it's called *Tomorrow's World* – no, no, it can't be, fat-head, *Yesterday's World* is what it's called, of course, *Yesterday's World* – what's disconcerting about *Yesterday's World* is its reticence. He divorced his first wife, who evidently adored him, to marry his secretary, who also evidently adored him, but you have no sense of a marrying and divorcing man in the autobiography, I don't mean in the citing of personal facts, I mean in the communication of a living and contradictory self – he speaks for civilisation, it's almost saintly, his voice, in its modest and humane authority – he knew every famous writer, musician, artist, and he describes them all with meticulous kindness and sensitivity, with what one could call, I suppose, a writer's eye, and yet they seem to fade from view even as you're reading – you don't think for a minute that he's lying, exactly, just that he's too well trained in himself to tell – or perhaps see, or sniff – the coarser grain, the tackier substance of the inner life of others, so it's really the authorised autobiography, and you have to feel your way behind its impeccable surface to realise what a sad and wounded and lost creature he must have been when he wrote it – and then you realise that the surface is itself the achievement, without it he couldn't have written at all about his times, the early ones and their charms, and then the later ones and their horrors, which for him could have no end, his world was over – and don't forget – don't forget what? Have I time to remember? Remember what?

Oh yes, yes, and there's his biography of Balzac, he thought of it as his life's great work although it was still unfinished at his death – but even unfinished and in translation it's a quite wonderful book, free and easy in its manner – the extravagant French genius who died of coffee, overwork and above all crazy impulses, falling hopelessly in love with women who wrote him fan letters, stalking them with sexual yearning and urgency until he was humiliated by them or tired of them, often first one and then the other – all his sexual and emotional luck came when he was a very young man, with good and experienced older women who made love to him and mothered him – yes, Zweig tells it all with charm and zest and something more – a joy in celebrating a man who was, I would think, temperamentally his opposite – so – so there's his biography of Balzac and of course his novel *Beware of Pity*, two books for a writer to be proud of – he was a good and honourable man, I think, in ways which we no longer know much about, but finally no man can speak for the turmoil of his time unless he speaks from the turmoil of himself –

Victoria again. Time to go. Right. I must have a pee first. When I come back I'll write about Zweig's account of Balzac's marriage to the ghastly Madame Hanska and of his grotesque death, Zweig tells it superbly, the pathetic and the farcical in perfect balance – no, no I won't, I'll simply write down what Dr Rootle says, and whatever it is, that had better be the end of this, this whatever it is, they will be my last words, my last written words on the subject of myself – off you go – I've only smoked three cigarettes today, will that be taken into account? Off, off you go, off we go.

## I Fall in Love

I haven't been here doing this for four days, since the morning of the day that we went to see Dr Rootle, to get the result of the scan, and to find out what my immediate future would be. I don't know why I've postponed writing about it, it almost feels like a moral lapse, a kind of laziness. I've pulled the pad towards me, picked up my pen, I see I actually wrote a few words, in such a scrawl that I'm still not sure I can read them correctly, but I think they are: 'He came into the waiting room and went to the receptionist's desk directly behind us.'

I can't remember much before that, all the business of getting to the hospital, finding the right area – oh, I do remember it wasn't the usual hospital, it was somewhere even nearer to us, it took almost no time to get there, and then we – what? Yes, we walked about outside for a few minutes, then went into the lobby, which was like a combination of a Hilton Hotel and an airport departure lounge, people sitting on sofas and on chairs in postures of attention, hands on their knees and leaning forward, or whispering to their partners, as if waiting for their flight to be called – there were lots of Arabs, I remember, outnumbering the other patients – we went to one of the reception desks and were told that Dr Rootle's office was downstairs in the basement. As we were early we hung about where we were. I had several pees in a clean and comfortable lavatory, nervous pees or rather pees from nervousness, and I thought, as I always do in tense situations, first nights and such, that I must be careful not to dribble down my trousers or over my shoes – I would have been wearing espadrilles, as I've worn them all week, dark blue espadrilles, I doubt if they'd have shown any stains but of course one can't be too careful, one wants to be at one's most self-possessed when receiving life/death-type news.

When we had five minutes to go we went down in the lift to the basement and – and it was a small waiting room, there were only three or four people sitting about, I don't remember anything about them or much else until – try and pick up from the one sentence I wrote down – 'He came into the waiting room and went to the receptionist's desk directly behind us.' Yes, that's right. He came out of a door that opened on to the waiting room, so there he was, suddenly, abruptly really, one second walking towards us, and seemingly smiling a welcome so that I stood up, and then he was past us, at the counter and talking to the receptionist in a low voice, so I sat down again, and then he was around in front of us, and I was on my feet again and he was shaking Victoria's hand, then mine, and he led us into his office, where we sat on two hard-backed chairs facing his desk, and he stood behind it, looking down at a folder, my folder I assumed, took out what looked like an X-ray, my scan I assumed, then sat down. He put the scan back into the folder and smiled, a huge smile as he has huge teeth, huge and white, that could make you feel like Little Red Riding Hood.

What followed was very confusing, and I can't recall, though I've tried, the exact words. In fact I have an idea that I didn't understand them, nor did Victoria, and we looked at one another for help. Part of the problem was Dr Rootle's manner, it seemed playful, almost teasing, his eyes sparkled and bulged behind his spectacles, and his teeth continued to flash – he looked more than ever like a large schoolboy – and then we realised, almost simultaneously, that he thought we knew the results of the scan – we said no, no, that's why we were here, to be told the results. He looked surprised, slightly disbelieving, but then our own surprise must have persuaded him that we weren't teasing him back. He didn't stop smiling as he explained that the scan showed that the radiotherapy had shrunk both tumours, furthermore there were no signs that the cancer had spread – although there was no question but that the cancer was still there, in the blood, and would eventually return. There were two ways of dealing with someone in my situation, the American way, which was to press on immediately with aggressive treatment, probably an intensive course of chemotherapy, which might prolong my life but perhaps by no more than a month or so, and would be very uncomfortable, if not downright miserable. The second way was the way that they favoured in this hospital, the English way, so to speak, which was to encourage the patient to lead as full a life as possible for as long as possible, and not to resort to intensive chemotherapy until it was absolutely necessary – towards the end, in other words, which in my case might be as far away as eighteen months or even two years. What did I think? I thought that I was in love with Dr Rootle, he was the most delightful man I'd ever met, I adored him, but I didn't say so. I said instead that it was better news than I'd dared hope. And then thought, let's get out of here now, immediately, no need to prolong the conversation into qualifications and so forth. I stood up and held out my hand. He shook it, then shook Victoria's hand, and came around the desk to open the door for us. I noticed that he didn't put his hand on my shoulder or clasp and squeeze my elbow, which I took to be a confirmation that I was out of the compassion zone for eighteen months or even two years – two whole – Victoria drove us home. I've no idea what we said. We were both in a kind of stupor – I mean, two years, two whole – well, eighteen months then, yes, let's keep it at eighteen months, in order to avoid disappointment.

# Acknowledgements

My thanks to

Ian Jack, for the time and care he has given to my memoirs, and for the great pleasure of his company

Dinah Wood, the editor of my plays, unfailing in her support and encouragement

Hugh Whitemore, always one of the first and most valuable readers of my writings

three true friends.